2
2/27

Field Hockey
Understanding the Game
2022

CRISTOPHER MALONEY

DEDICATION

To my late wife Barbara and our children
Sarah, Nick, Victoria, Bian, and Kiet

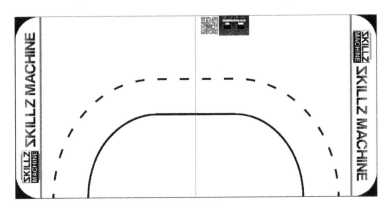

CONTENTS

Preface   i

1   The Sport of Hockey   1

2   Umpiring as a Window   47

3   Fairness vs. Safety   68

4   Understanding Umpire Signals   72

5   Understanding the Rules   93

6   Do You Know Enough to Umpire   215

7   How Did THAT Umpire Get THIS Game   221

8   Umpires on Game Day   228

9   Breaking Ties   254

10   Keeping Stats   258

11   Wisdom   275

12   Final Whistle and Quiz   281

13   Resources   288

PREFACE

A common, and oddly accepted, lament heard at field hockey games goes something like this, *"I've been watching field hockey for 10 years and I still don't understand it."* Trust me. Field hockey just isn't all THAT complicated and this book, while absolutely not a rule book, will help players, coaches, fans, reporters, and umpires better understand the game.

Most sports we learn by playing, slowly acquiring knowledge about the rules as we play. If one doesn't have any playing experience (or years of television coverage) to fall back on, the first thing they will probably ask when watching a sport for the first time is, "What are the rules?"

Even some of the most basic rules in a sport like football, which many of us seem to understand as if born with the knowledge implanted into our brains, take a great deal of explaining.

"You only get four downs to make a first down and you have to go 10 yards to get a first down."

If you know football, your reaction to that might just be, *"Duh."* However, if you don't know what 'down' means, that sentence will make absolutely no sense at all. *Activity: Try teaching someone what a down is in football.*

My overall intention is that this book is suitable for everyone involved or interested in learning more about the sport of hockey.

In helping you understand field hockey, I could have written this book from any number of different perspectives.

As I contemplated how to help people truly understand the sport of field hockey, I deter-mined that there are basically three approaches I could take.

ONE: Teach readers how to play the game – how to hold the stick, how to pass, etc. That approach is covered in my book *Field Hockey: The Beginner's Guide*. There are also numerous books with hundreds of drill patterns that coaches can use to help change their practice routines but, while one can gain an understanding of what players are asked to do to prepare for games, they don't necessarily help people understand the game.

TWO: Describe the game from a coaching perspective. How much time to spend on fitness training, individual stick skill development, how to transition out of the defensive end, what to do in the midfield, how best to attack the goal, etc., etc.

THREE: Provide readers with an understanding of the game from how the sport is umpired. In that way, you would learn about the rules and better understand what you see happening during a contest.

In the end, I decided that approaching the game with the understanding needed by umpires would be unique and best, rather than a "how to" guide. After all, to truly understand the game, you're going to need to know why the whistle is blown, not how players are taught how to pass the ball. You're going to need to know what the signals are that the umpire is using during the game, not what a goalkeeper thinks about when clearing the ball. You'll also want to know which umpire is responsible for what calls and why, not the drills teams do to attack or defend as a unit.

This is similar to how one truly understands football, basketball, and baseball. Seriously, can you understand football if you don't know the rules about the number of downs a team gets?

Understanding field hockey is complicated because, unlike in other countries, there are three different sets of rules governing play in the USA.

Globally, hockey is governed by the *Rules of Hockey*, which is published by the world hockey authority International Hockey Federation (FIH). In the USA, in addition to the *Rules of Hockey*, two other sets of rules are used.

Hockey played between high schools in the USA is almost always governed by the National Federation of State High School Associations (NFHS). Hockey played between colleges is governed by the National Collegiate Athletic Association (NCAA). The *Rules of Hockey* govern everyone else.

None of the modifications to the *Rules of Hockey* made by the NFHS or NCAA impact how a person officiates but there are times when rule differences change which penalty the umpire is expected to apply. This can be confusing for players, coaches, fans, <u>and</u> umpires when they move between games played under different rules.

How in the world does a born-and-raised American male start playing hockey? Let me tell you...

In my first year at college (September 1975), I began hitting the ball around with friends on the college hockey team. Within a few weeks, I was playing with a local men's club team. Vonnie Gros, head coach of the USA's 1980 and 1984 Olympic Women's Field Hockey Team, invited me to practice with the varsity hockey team at West Chester University, my alma mater. I practiced with the team every day during my years at WCU. I began officiating in 1976, while I was in college. In order to actually play in games, I made weekly trips from WCU and my hometown (Moorestown, NJ) to Washington, DC and New York, NY to play on various men's teams. Playing time was often limited so, more often than not, I ended up officiating games for the teams in the league.

My career as a competitive player ended after I played for the East Team in the USOC's 1982 National Sports Festival (silver medal). I was coaching high school hockey at the time and decided that the commitment of being a potential Olympic-level athlete didn't square with my interests in getting married, which I did in 1983, and starting a family. My oldest daughter, Sarah, was born during the opening ceremonies of the 1984 Olympics. On June 1, 2011, Sarah was in the delivery room again, only this time she was the one giving birth to her first child, Aaron. My wife and I, along with Sarah's three younger siblings, Nick, Victoria, and Bian, entered a new phase in the family's growth.

In 1981, I organized a local mixed league primarily of high school age boys and girls. Three of the boys in that league went on to compete in the USOC's 1985 Olympic Festival (formerly the National Sports Festival). I organized and ran the process used that year to select the East Team. I was selected to serve as the team's assistant coach. The team was undefeated and won the gold medal. One of the boys from my mixed league set an Olympic Festival scoring record (his nickname was Gorilla); another scored the winning goal in the gold medal game, and a third was the team's goalkeeper. The goalkeeper, Steve Wagner, Mt. Laurel, NJ, went on to become the goalkeeper for the USA's Men's Team and played for the team in the 1996 Olympics.

In 1983, I founded the Garden State Games Field Hockey Event (part of the "Olympics" for athletes in the state of New Jersey) and served as the event's director for many years. In its second year, the GSGFH Event became the first annual hockey event in the country to be held on a synthetic surface.

In 1985, the national governing body for hockey in the USA invited me to participate in an International Olympic Committee international solidarity seminar for hockey coaching. The course director was Richard Aggis, former coach of the Australian national team. I was asked to present my paper entitled *Field Hockey: The First Thirty Minutes*. While there are many specific tactics a team can use in the first thirty minutes of a hockey game, this presentation wasn't about those thirty minutes. It was borne out of a learned necessity to quickly teach new players (males) how to play hockey in less than thirty minutes—often for a game that would be starting in less than thirty minutes. The approach has proven to be a very good way to teach all beginners how to get off to a successful start.

In 1986, I again served as a coach at the USOC's Olympic Festival and, happily, that team also was undefeated and won the gold medal. The Olympic Festival should not be confused with the National Hockey Festival, an annual club event put on by USA Field Hockey.

I worked as the stadium and play-by-play announcer at three USOC Olympic Festivals and at several international tournaments. Most recently, I was the play-by-play announcer for a World League Tournament, the webcasts of Princeton University's home games, and the Metro Atlantic Athletic Conference Championships. Most recently, I was the play-by-play and color announcer for the Men's and Women's 2021 Indoor Hockey Pan Am Cup.

I remained actively involved with hockey throughout the 1990's serving as the director of the USA Field Hockey's Futures program in New Jersey and coaching in the program for many years. During this time I continued to officiate, calling men's club games and competitions at the high school and college level, Division I and III.

In 2001, the president of a local umpire association asked me to provide training to the association's umpires. Luckily, with older children and the flexibility afforded to me by current career pursuits, I was able to once again become involved with hockey!

Although I continue to play socially and officiate competitive hockey, most of my focus in the last decade has been spent advancing hockey through the development of umpires and presentation of rules education programs to players, coaches, and fans.

In 2002, I began publishing UmpireHockey.com. Through UmpireHockey.com, I have been able to reach a broad, English-language audience with precise and accurate information—including videos— concerning hockey officiating. In the USA, the site helped to address and eliminate "rules" that would more accurately be labeled as "rumors" that negatively influence the way hockey was being officiated. Very often, hockey umpires are left to deal with the results of the uninformed, informing the even more uninformed. UmpireHockey.com helps bridge the gap between the austere nature with which the *Rules of Hockey* must be written and a layman's misunderstandings. The site also serves as an advocate for umpires.

The year before UmpireHockey.com was launched I began teaching pre-teen and young teenagers how to officiate hockey; actively recruiting players to begin officiating. This is not, generally, an accepted practice in the USA. In fact, most umpire associations in the USA still ban membership to those under-18 years of age. A bias against youngsters officiating is deeply entrenched in the hockey officiating culture throughout most of the USA.

In the spring of 2005 many of the teenagers who had been participating in a training program I developed and called "JUMP IN!" officiated at USA Field Hockey's Regional Futures Tournament held in New Jersey. Some went on to officiate at the Garden State Games Field Hockey Event. By the fall of 2005, in my area (central New Jersey) we had two 14-year olds certified and officiating interscholastic hockey games. USA Field Hockey decided to use the program I ran in the New Jersey regional tournament as a model for expanding this development effort throughout the country in 2006. In what turned out to be the single largest response to recruit new umpires, more than 100 athletes volunteered to officiate at 11 regional tournaments. Sadly, the efforts to develop teenage umpires did not immediately continue. Why? At the time, those in umpire leadership positions in the 11 regions were part of the aforementioned culture with a bias against the development of young umpires.

To ensure I am as up-to-date as possible in the information I teach and publish, I continually upgrade my knowledge of hockey officiating and, that is something all umpires should do—or retire.

In 2002 and 2003, I attended national interpretation meetings held respectively in Maryland and Massachusetts. In the summer of 2005, I matriculated into the National Umpire Course offered by USA Field Hockey. The instructor was the late Jane Nockolds, an umpire from England who represented Great Britain as an umpire at the Olympics and World Cup women's tournaments and is on the FIH List of Outdoor Hockey Umpires Managers. Later in the year, USA Field Hockey held its first-ever certification course for Umpire Coaches. Thirty-six umpires from across the country were invited to participate and I was honored to be among those invited and earn this new national certification. Don Prior, an umpire from Australia who represented Australia as an umpire at two Olympic and World Cup gold medal games, was the instructor. In June of 2008, I was re-certified as one of USA Field Hockey's umpire coaches.

Though much of what Ms. Nockolds and Mr. Prior presented was similar, there were significant differences in certain aspects of the way they manage any given game. For example, Ms. Nockolds presented that on the third early break by the defense on a Penalty Corner, a Penalty Stroke should be awarded as long as she's given the defense ample visual and verbal warning so no one is surprised. How does she warn the defenders? On the second break she stands in front of the defense, shakes her head and indicates "No," with hand signals and, finally, illustrates that if the defense breaks again she will award a Penalty Stroke. While presenting these visual signals she is, at the same time, talking with the defenders to help them understand that she will, absolutely, award a Penalty Stroke if they break early again. The verbal is for the defenders; the visual not only serves to emphasize her words to the defenders but also provides "fair warning" to everyone in the stadium the consequences of another early break.

Mr. Prior also talks with the players, encouraging them not to leave early, but said he would never award a Penalty Stroke for early breaks but instead green card a defender on the second break and then start yellow carding players for each subsequent break—one after another—confident that the defending team would quote, *"Get the message."*

I prefer to follow Mr. Prior's advice on this because it fits better with my own philosophy that we charge individuals with personal penalties rather than risk the immediate potential of putting a team behind by a goal because of one player's misconduct—even if such action might have been the team's strategy.

Do I have to consider Ms. Nockolds wrong because my philosophy dictates that I take a different approach? No. Both Ms. Nockolds' and Mr. Prior's decisions were supported by the rules and then current interpretations. Even though I disagree with Ms. Nockolds's final action, her approach made it absolutely clear what she was going to do and then, most important, she did exactly what she promised. Let's face it, in truth, Ms. Nockolds doesn't give the defense the Penalty Stroke—the defense gives itself the Penalty Stroke.

These two correct approaches by two of the top umpires in the world speak to the ever-challenging environment in which people officiate.

In 2008, I founded Captain of the Year, Inc. (www.CaptainAward.org), a nonprofit corporation that recognizes student-athletes who demonstrate excellent rules knowledge, sportsmanship, and leadership. The organization hopes to improve the relationships between players and umpires.

Although I had for many years been working on various umpiring programs for USA Field Hockey, that work was completed anonymously. That changed in 2009 when it was announced that I was the technical editor for the RULES and UMPIRES sections of USAFieldHockey.com, including the *Ask The Umpire* feature. In 2010, I became the interim editor for all of USAFieldHockey.com and began directing the National Rules Briefings for USA Field Hockey (indoor and outdoor rules).

In 2011, I formed the Ocean Atlantic Field Hockey Association in conjunction with USA Field Hockey's development initiative for boys' field hockey (OAFHA.org and BoysFieldHockey.com). I serve the organization as its technical director for player and umpire training.

In 2012, the OAFHA began hosting a USA Field Hockey program for boys and girls between 7 and 14 years of age called FUNdamentals.

In the summer of 2013, the OAFHA launched a Hockey5s league (Hockey5s.com) to provide playing opportunities for children, older teenagers, and adults. The games feature simplified rules and offer excellent 'real world' experience for new umpires.

Later in the year I completed my second book, *JUMP IN! A Beginner's Guide To Field Hockey Umpiring*, which was commissioned by and is available from USA Field Hockey.

In 2014, I proposed that USA Field Hockey change the name of Indoor Hockey for boys to Ricochet Hockey and make three rule changes. The first would allow scoring from anywhere on the court. The second would eliminate Penalty Corners and Penalty Strokes, replacing both with the Challenge from Hockey5s.

I also introduced the idea of Juggernaut Field Hockey in 2014. It's a development idea that mirrors the interest many high schools have in holding a 'counter-culture' Powder Puff Football game between the Senior and Junior girls.

Juggernaut Field Hockey would tap into that same 'counter-culture' sensibility and could feature Senior boys versus the Junior boys (and perhaps other underclassmen) in a field hockey game held to raise money for charity, perhaps to help fight prostate cancer.

In 2015, I began formalizing Super6s (Super6s.com), an exciting, fast-paced version of field hockey. It is a cross-field, score-from-anywhere, action-packed, 6v6 game. Super6s gives participants 10 times the number of hockey touches and decision making opportunities than a full-field, 11v11 game. It a great version of the sport for umpires and new players as there are no Penalty Corners.

In late September of 2016, I released the High-Performance Umpiring & Current Rules™ course available completely online. Within four months there were students enrolled from Boston, Massachusetts to Ann Arbor, Michigan. The global potential of the initiative proved real when a student from Uganda signed up before the end of the year. Two NFHS umpire associations, one in Massachusetts and one in New Jersey, made the course their official umpire training course. Within one year, more than 150 people in 20 USA states and 5 countries have signed up to complete the course.

In 2017, I organized an all-boys field hockey team and traveled to numerous tournaments in Pennsylvania and New Jersey. The boys were all under 10-years old and from the same NJ county. Perhaps this bodes well for the future of our sport in the USA.

In 2018, I published *Field Hockey: The Beginner's Guide*. The book provides a broad overview of the sport and helpful "how to" details for beginners and those new to the sport. Designed with many large photographs and illustrations, the book has been well received by readers.

In 2019, I published *Field Hockey: How a Boy Won the Right to Play*. The book includes the 29-page judgment in favor of a high school boy in New Jersey who wanted to play on his school's only field hockey team. He brought a case against his school and the New Jersey State Interscholastic Athletic Association (NJSIAA). The book includes an analysis of the judgment. Witnesses whose statements were referenced in the judgment included those of the executive directors of the NJSIAA, the Massachusetts Interscholastic Athletic Association (MIAA), Richard Kentwell, and myself.

In 2020, I created three training aids – the Hockey Hammer (an illegally heavy stick weighing ~850 grams), the BubbaBall (an illegally heavy ball weighing ~210 grams), and the DinoBall (an illegally heavy ball weighing ~475 grams). All are designed to help increase hand, wrist, and arm strength, and improve a player's pushing and flicking skills.

It is my hope that this book and the online umpiring course will contribute to the advancement of the sport.

I would enjoy hearing from you. My email address is:

cris.maloney@gmail.com (no H in Cris)

REVIEWS / ENDORSEMENTS APPRECIATED
After reading this book, you are encouraged to leave a review with your local bookseller or on Amazon.com.

CHAPTER 1

THE SPORT OF HOCKEY

The Game

In a description designed to be brutish, hockey is a game that allows 22 athletes (11 per team) to run around smacking a ball with three-foot clubs carried in their hands. The basic objective is to bang a rock-hard ball into the other team's goal. The winning team is the one that was most successful at scoring goals (each goal = one point). A heavily padded goalkeeper protects their team's goal. The goal mouth is 12 feet wide and 7 feet high. This goes on for an hour, with short rest periods during the battle, after which the teams change directions and attack the goal that they were previously defending. Two umpires officiate the contest.

QUESTION: **Why don't field hockey umpires switch ends when the teams switch ends?**

ANSWER: **The umpires remain in their relative positions so each team's attack and defense has 'the other umpire' for an equal amount of time.**

The loutish description above may well be an apt account of a game between novice teams. In the hands of skilled athletes, practiced in the sport, a hockey stick becomes a tool no less refined than a surgeon's scalpel. An attacking team tries to dissect the opponent's defense utilizing geometric attack patterns created in classroom settings, perfected after hours and hours of practice, and executed with finesse and uncanny precision on a 60 yard by 100 yard surface specifically designed for hockey competitions. These superbly fit individual performers demonstrate grace under pressure, exquisite timing while competing at extraordinary speed, brilliant instinctive reactions to unpredictable circumstances, calm during head-to-head challenges, and finishing set plays requiring a seemingly clairvoyant connection between teammates.

Coaches use various team structures…

- 5-3-2-GK
- 4-2-3-1-GK
- 3-3-3-1-GK

…and different attacking and defending strategies depending upon the abilities of their athletes and those of the opponents.

The History

A drawing found in tombs at Beni-Hasen in the Nile Valley of Egypt depicts men playing hockey some 4,000 years ago. The modern game has its roots in England where it was once banned by a king who felt the men were spending too much time playing and not enough time preparing for battles (later another king of England ordered that all the sticks in the country be burned for the same reason).

Interestingly enough, it was the British army that introduced the game across the globe via the British colonies, leading to the first official international competition in 1895.

A physical education instructor from England, Constance Applebee, introduced the sport to women in the USA when she was attending a seminar at Harvard University in 1901.

Photograph of Constance Applebee taken by my umpiring friend Genya Pantuso.

Hockey has been part of the Olympics since 1908 for men and for women since 1980. In 1980 the USA Women's National Team had high hopes for an Olympic gold medal but those dreams were dashed when President Jimmy Carter announced that the USA would not participate in the 1980 Olympic Games, which were held in Moscow, because the Soviet Union had invaded Afghanistan.

Today, only soccer and possibly cricket are more popular than hockey in terms of worldwide participation. Further, only in the

USA and Canada do more women play hockey than men.

NOTE: More men play field hockey than football (American football) and baseball combined.

Historic Changes to Hockey

Until 2008, one of the most interesting changes in the modern history of the game was the elimination of the off-sides rule. In 2008 the Euro Hockey League (www.ehlhockey.tv) created a new rule that allowed the athlete restarting play (on a Free Hit, side-in, etc.) to do so with a self-pass. In 2009 the Hockey Rules Board (named the FIH Rules Committee in 2011) refined the EHL's creation and the FIH published a mandatory experimental rule similar to the EHL's. The rule was added a year later to the NFHS rules governing games between high schools in the USA. The action of restarting play by passing to oneself is fairly unique in sport and has radically changed how the game is played. In 2012 the rule was modified again, eliminating the requirement to pass to oneself, which required the player to begin with two separate actions. Now, no separation is needed and I wish the FIH would drop the "pass" from self-pass and call it a self-start.

The self-start also changed how umpires officiate. In the old days umpires were taught to stop after whistling so the athletes could easily find the umpire to see what primary signal the umpire was showing. Now, the umpires must continue to move in order to maintain the best possible line of sight to the play— a position from which to make the best possible calls.

Also of note, especially to those of you returning to the game of hockey from ages ago, are changes to how obstruction and foot contact with the ball is being called.

While many people believe that the obstruction rule has never changed, and that only the interpretation has gone through dramatic changes, that's not true. The obstruction rule has changed. In the old days, umpires called obstruction "turning" and if a player with the ball turned, it was considered a violation. Coaches in America actually used to tell the players on their teams to, *"Keep your feet pointing toward your goal,"* in desperate attempts to teach their players not to violate the dreaded 'turning' rule.

The modern obstruction rule allows an attacker with the ball to spin like a top, run around in circles, dribble through his or her legs, standstill, or turn and dribble away, and never be in violation of the obstruction rule. What players cannot do is to actually, purposefully, actively make use of their body or stick in such a way that will keep a nearby opponent, who is actually, actively trying to reach the ball, from being able to play the ball.

In the 2003-04 fall season, one of the last vestiges of this old interpretation at the high school level in the USA fell when the NFHS (finally) eliminated the 'turning' signal for obstruction and replaced it with the obstruction signal as published in the *Rules of Hockey* – arms crossed in front of chest like an X with palms toward umpire's body.

Further, the rule involving contact between the foot and ball has been refined. It's one thing for the athlete to kick the ball; it's another if an athlete's foot is hit by the ball. As long as the opponent was not disadvantaged, the umpire does not blow the whistle simply because the ball and foot come into contact with each other.

Other rules have changed since the time that I started officiating in 1977.

First, goalkeepers and field players are now allowed to play a ball that is above their shoulders.

Second, players are now allowed to use the edge (call it the side) of their sticks. The rule didn't change. What happened was that the definition of the flat side of the stick was expanded to include the edges of the stick.

Third, goalkeepers were given permission to use their non-stick hand to play the ball away from an attacker with a scoring opportunity. The year before that last change, if the goalkeeper moved the ball with their non-stick hand, a Penalty Stroke would be called—now, it's *"Play on!"*

Fourth, the Corner (a.k.a. the Long Hit) has been removed from the *Rules of Hockey* and NFHS games. Now, when the ball crosses outside the field of play via the back-line when last touched by the defense (and it wasn't played over the back-line intentionally), rather than being placed on the side-line near the corner, the ball is placed on the 23-meter line in front of where the ball went out of bounds.

Fifth, goalkeepers and field players are allowed play a ball while it is above their shoulders – as high as they can reach, even if that includes jumping off the ground. This makes the game safer as players who try to lift the ball over their opponents must now lift the ball WAY OVER the heads of their opponents to be successful (i.e. fewer head-bound hockey balls).

An important change launched at the 1976 Olympics in Montreal, Canada, was the introduction of artificial surfaces. No other non-rule change in the sport had as big an impact as when the FIH began holding all international competitions on artificial surfaces. Now widely available in the USA at the high school level and the dominant surface used in intercollegiate games, "turf" has changed the tactics of the game, the approach to training, the skills that are possible, and the level of fitness umpires have to bring to each game.

The introduction of turf caused a shift in the world's hockey powers, away from India and Pakistan and towards Australia, Germany, Great Britain, and The Netherlands. I predict that the introduction of the self-pass may help return India and Pakistan to prominence. One thing that has already come true is that umpires need a much higher level of physical fitness to maintain proper position.

Changes to equipment have revolutionized the goalkeeping position and transformed stick skills.

Finally, players have changed. They're training year round, they're faster and stronger, and they're developing higher level skills at younger and younger ages—yet more reasons umpires have to maintain a higher level of fitness than ever before.

If a field hockey umpire who learned how to officiate a decade or so ago thinks that because they know the new rules they don't have to change, they are not being at all realistic.

Let's take a look outside of field hockey. As I mentioned earlier, I started officiating in 1976. In the 1976 Olympics the winning time in the men's 100 meter dash was 10.06 seconds. The winning time for the women that year was 11.08 seconds. Running those times today, neither of those Olympic gold medalists would even come close to taking home the bronze. The same dramatic changes are evident in swimming.

Ten years after I started officiating, devoted high school age athletes played field hockey about three months a year. In early August, some players would attend "captain practices". Many teams would go to an overnight camp in the middle of August. The season would start in early September and end for most teams by the first few days of November. The number of playing days college-bound field hockey players participate in has radically changed .

Playing Opportunities (old days versus nowadays)

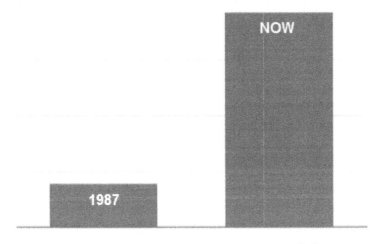

See opportunity details at UmpireHockey.com/playing

In the winter, devoted high school age players play on club

teams and compete in local, regional, and national indoor tournaments.

In the spring, they practice with the club team, play in spring tournaments, and many participate on weekends in a USA Field Hockey program started in the early 1990's called Futures. In the summer they continue playing with their club teams and many compete in local, state, regional, and national tournaments. In August, they attend summer camps just like the players in 1987 did but now, many of the counselors/instructors are men and women coming from overseas and so the skills they learn are often exciting ones they've never seen before. Then, of course, they use these newly acquired skills while playing for their school team during the traditional fall hockey season, which for most players goes into the second week of November.

To top things off, just before starting indoor hockey again, many play on their club team in the USA Field Hockey's National Hockey Festival—the largest field hockey tournament in the world.

Because the game is constantly changing, be skeptical when someone like me asserts themselves into a conversation about the rules by telling you they've been officiating for more than 30 years. The follow-up question should be, *"How much have you been changing?"* In short, officiating experience is worthless if the umpire officiates today like they did when they started officiating 30 years ago.

The Latest Big Change

Before 2016, when the attack restarted play inside the attacking 23-meter area, the ball could be played into the circle after it traveled 5 meters or was touched by a defender or a second attacker. I call these the requirements of Indirect Circle Entry (ICE) because many years ago the attacker used to be able to play the ball directly into the circle from a restart anywhere on the competition surface.

Changes to the *Rules of Hockey* that allow a restart to take place within 5 meters of the circle (rather than being forced to first place the ball 5 meters from the circle before restarting play) exposed an interesting opportunity to attacking teams.

To take advantage of a restart taking place near the edge of the circle, the attacking team would put the ball into play with a small movement and a teammate would sprint to the ball from a position that was 5 meters away and hit the ball hard into the circle. The play sent the ball into the circle at a high velocity in hopes of finding a defender's foot (and the award of an attacking Penalty Corner). This was a dangerous action and circumvented the very reason for the ICE requirements.

Now, the criteria for meeting the requirements of ICE do not include a second attacker. Before being played into the circle, the ball from a restart within the attacking 23-meter area, must travel 5 meters or be touched by a defender. There is no mention of a second attacker. If the ball has not traveled 5 meters or is not touched by a defender before it enters the circle, it is a breach and possession is awarded to the defense.

QUESTION: **How does a good umpire keep current?**

ANSWER: **They study the rules every year, attend an annual briefing, take a certification course every four years, and they remain ever willing to change.**

Embracing Change

It is important to understand that hockey does change. Even though this book is updated annually, it is possible that rules discussed in this book have been changed since the time the book was published.

Umpires, coaches, and players must agree to be open-minded about changes in the sport. Someday all participants must be one of two things—either an old dog that can learn new tricks or retired because they can't learn new tricks. The following have undergone major changes since I began playing in 1975:

- Surface (game is faster)

- Off-sides (eliminated)

- Players (they are faster, stronger, better)

- Self-Pass (game is faster)

- Indirect Circle Entry (more umpiring decisions)

- Obstruction (almost requires physical contact)

- Permissible Stick Skills (edge play and play above shoulders)

- Corner (eliminated)

How could I possibly participate today, if I weren't eager to change with the game? An umpire, for example, who doesn't remain fit and change with the times is a detriment to the game. They demonstrate their lack of commitment to the players and the sport by losing mobility and not changing. Having these umpires available to officiate games isn't helping anyone, let alone the game of hockey. Now, imagine if coaches didn't change their approach to the game when the rules change.

The Competition Surface

You probably cannot imagine a basketball game being allowed to be played on a court covered with an inch of water. Why then do parents sit back and allow field hockey games to be to be played on surfaces like these...

I believe the answer is that the parents don't understand the game. They don't know that they should take action.

Parents should make sure that if a school provides a basketball court that is free of bumps and divots, that the school provide a flat surface for their children's hockey games. If the school can't install a synthetic competition surface for hockey, then the grass should be cut to ½ inch on game days and the surface should be rolled with a 600 to 700 pound roller at least once a week.

The best surface for hockey is synthetic. Even competition surfaces on grass that are fertilized and mowed are typically so negatively impacted by weather events (freezing, thawing, flooding, drought, etc.) that they become impractical for hockey competitions UNLESS the surface is also rolled. Grass surfaces given additional and extraordinary (read that "expensive") care can be cured of their ills and made ready for hockey.

Grass Height

The NFHS has a rule (Rule 1, Section 2, Article 1) that states that grass "should" be cut to a maximum height of 1½ inches. In short (no pun intended), the worst case scenario is that grass should not be taller than 1½ inches on game day. Even then half of the ball is hidden—more when the ball drops into a space between clumps of grass. Tall grass creates a dangerous playing environment and games should be postponed when the competition surface is dangerous.

 UMPIRES: If grass on a competition surface exceeds 1.5" in height, you "should" postpone the game.

PARENTS: **A school cannot cut the grass to a legal height on a Monday for a game being played two or three days later and think they've met the requirements of the rule. Show the AD at your kid's school the images on the next page and discuss why the grounds crew preparing the competition surface should "underperform" the rule. A typical objection is that doing so will kill the grass. It won't, as long as it is watered. I know you think coaches and umpires complain about long grass but, they don't. If they do, they get fired.**

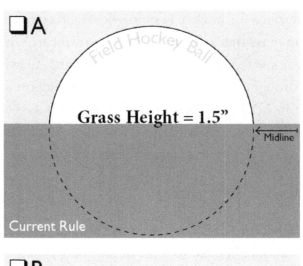

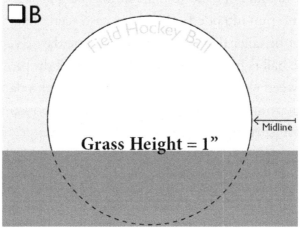

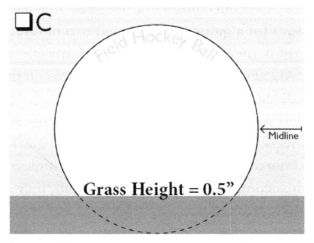

The Competition Surface and Goals

The hockey competition surface is most often called a "field" in America. I don't like using the word field to describe the surface on which athletes are supposed to compete in a surface sport like hockey.

I grew up on a farm and I learned that we grow corn and raise cows in a field. Some of the hockey fields I've officiated on do look like cow pastures. Calling a hockey field the "competition surface" sends a more compelling message to those who care for and prepare the "field" and helps remind people that hockey games need to take place on surfaces suitable for an athletic competition—which is a higher calling than a surface suitable for cows and corn.

I realize that there are still many aspects of the sport where the word "field" is used. For example, "open field play" and "a mid-fielder" and "a field player" but, when talking specifically about the surface on which the game is played, please get into the habit of calling it the competition surface.

The boundaries of a properly marked competition surface are 55 meters (60 yards) by 91.4 meters (100 yards). The competition surface extends for 5 meters beyond each boundary line so the game can be properly officiated. This is the area from where umpires often have to go in order to maintain proper positioning relative to the play (which is not to say that umpires must always be outside the playing area). The long and "wide" of it, therefore, is that the space needed to hold a competition is 70 yards wide by 110 yards long.

Listed below are some basics about the competition surface and the goals, however, reviewing the diagrams in the rule book for additional details will provide, well, additional details.

- Every marking on the competition surface is 3 inches wide

- The vertical posts and horizontal bar of the goals that face the competition surface are flat, at 90 degrees to the competition surface, and 2 inches wide. The sides of the front posts are 3 inches deep

- The internal dimensions of the goal's mouth are 7 feet tall by 12 feet wide. The goal is 4 feet deep at the bottom

- At the sides and back of the goal are the goal boards, sometimes called bottom boards. They must be 18 inches high and of a dark color (on the inside of the goal). Umpires use the height of the boards to help judge whether certain shots on Penalty Corners are legal

- The Penalty Stroke mark is in the scoring zone/circle, 7 yards in front of the center of goal line

- The "circle" is made up of two-quarter circles, each with a radius of 16 yards, drawn from each goal post and joined by a line parallel to and 16 yards away from the goal line

QUESTION: **How many goals are on a hockey field?**

ANSWER: **Zero. The goals are placed outside the playing area, behind the goal lines**

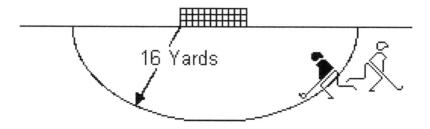

The Circle / The D / The Scoring Zone

The scoring zone is commonly known and referred to as the circle (as illustrated above, the attack player in black can score because the attacker has touched the ball inside the circle). Naturally, it is NOT the shape of a circle. It is more like the shape of the letter D. And, naturally, when one hears a coach tells his or her players to, *"Get back on D,"* the instruction never means to run into the circle, which is the shape of a D, but to get back on defense—a lot of which takes place in the circle. Are you with me?

There was a time that the NCAA decided to experiment with a rule that allowed the attack to score from anywhere within 23 meters of the entire back-line. The idea behind expanding the scoring zone was that it would lead to more goals making the game more exciting for fans. It didn't work. And, as I recall, immediately thereafter our women's national team, fueled by NCAA players, plummeted on the world stage.

Restarting Play

At the beginning of each period, after a goal, when there is a change of possession by an umpire's enforcement of the rules, or because the ball has gone out of bounds, play is restarted in one of the following ways:

1) Types of Free Hits (Starts/Restarts)

a) Period Start/Goal: Center Pass

At the beginning of each period and following each goal, the ball is placed in the middle of the competition surface. This is the only time in the game when all the players have to be on the half of the competition surface that their team is defending. Play may be restarted with any legal action – push, hit, lift, pass, or self-start (lifting and hitting is not allowed indoors).

b) Rule Breach

Team A breaks the rules giving team B possession. Play restarts near the point of the breach. Play may be restarted with any legal action – push, hit, lift, pass, or self-start (lifting and hitting is not allowed indoors). Indirect circle entry is required when the attack is awarded a free hit within the attacking 23-meter area.

c) Boundary Ball – Sideline: (Side-in)

A ball over the sideline. Play restarts where the ball crossed over the sideline. Play may be restarted with any legal action – push, hit, lift, pass, or self-start (lifting and hitting is not allowed indoors). Indirect circle entry is required when the attack will restart the ball within the attacking 23-meter area.

d) Boundary Ball – Back-line: Free Hit (attack) at the 23 (formerly "Corner", "Long Hit", and "Long Corner")

A ball over the back-line when touched last by the defender and the defender did not intentionally play the ball out of bounds. Play is restarted from the 23-meter line "in front" of where the ball crossed the back-line or the goal-line when a goal is not scored. Play may be restarted with any legal action – push, hit, lift, pass, or self-start (lifting and hitting is not allowed indoors). Indirect circle entry is required.

e) Boundary Ball – Back-line: Defense Ball ("16")

A ball over the back-line, last touched by attack. Play may be restarted on the back-line where it went out or as many as 16-yards away in front of where the ball crossed the back-line. Play may be restarted with any legal action – push, hit, lift, pass, or self-start (lifting and hitting is not allowed indoors).

2) Types of Penalties

a) Penalty Corner (slang: "Short Corner" and "Shortie")

The umpire penalizes the defense and awards the attack a Penalty Corner when the defense intentionally breaks the rules inside the 23-meter area (inside the half they are defending in indoor hockey). Penalty corners are also given when a rule is broken unintentionally by the defense occurring inside the circle if the foul had no direct consequence on a goal scoring opportunity. Further, when an indoor or outdoor defender, inside the circle or not, has possession of the ball and intentionally puts it over the back-line to keep the attack from getting it, the defense is penalized with a Penalty Corner.

b) Penalty Stroke

The umpire penalizes the defense with a Penalty Stroke when the defense commits an intentional breach inside the circle or whenever they illegally stop a sure goal. For example, if a defender slashes at and strikes the stick of an attacker who is about to shoot the ball or when an attacker's shot gets past the goalkeeper and is stopped from crossing the goal line by some part of another defender's body, a Penalty Stroke is awarded.

[NFHS: A Penalty Stroke is awarded when a coach earns a red card for a flagrant foul (12.1.PENALTIES.1.d).]

3) Oddity – The Bully

A bully takes place when an incident occurs that causes play to stop that is not part of a game action—for example, an umpire accidentally blows his/her whistle when play should have continued or a flock of geese lands on the competition surface. The bully takes place where the ball was when the event happened. If this takes place close to a boundary line, the ball is moved away from the line (14.6 meters/16 yards from the back-lines and 5 meters from the sidelines).

NOTE: If a bully is called interrupting a Penalty Corner, play is restarted by resetting the Penalty Corner.

The Stick

All sticks must be able to pass through a metal ring with an internal diameter of 51mm (2 inches). When athletes put tape on their stick, it oftentimes will fail to pass through the ring. A stick that does not pass through the ring is kept in the umpire's care until the end of the game. A stick ring fashioned from PVC piping or other non-metal material is NOT acceptable. Sticks must have a bow less than 25mm (0.98 inches).

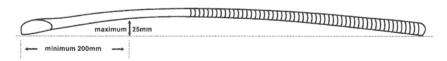

Sticks may not weigh more than 26 ounces (1.6 pounds). Sticks must be in relatively good repair so they would not be abrasive if a glancing contact were made, i.e. no splinters.

Umpires are not expected to weigh field hockey sticks. They are, however, expected to know the rules.

The striking end of all of the sticks is flat on the left side and round on the right. The ball may only be moved with the flat side of the stick, which includes both edges of the stick's "blade". This rule tends to give right-handed players a power advantage, and left-handed players an advantage in dribbling. Without a single-sided design, the game would feature right- and left-handed players finishing their swings into each other's faces.

The Athletes

Each outdoor team can put a maximum of 11 players in the competition during regulation time (6 players for indoor games). An opposing team is under no obligation to play with less than a full complement when one team plays with less than eleven players. The dress of the player is governed by the rules.

[NFHS (1.4.1): Teams MUST have a fully equipped goalkeeper in the game at all times. A team without a goalkeeper forfeits the game.

A high school team in the USA can compete with as few as seven players, as long as one is a fully kitted goalkeeper. It is also good to remember that while players competing in games between high schools in the USA can wear metal goggles, but the players are NOT allowed to wear jewelry, 'training posts', watches, soft bracelets, necklaces, face paint, barrettes, etc. In 2011, USA Field Hockey removed its banning of any and all jewelry but dangerous items can be "sent off" by the umpires. I did that once – a woman who wasn't wearing gloves was wearing an engagement ring with a very large diamond during an indoor game. I felt it was dangerous.]

The Field Player

STICK

When a good umpire asks a player for his or her stick so it can be checked and the athlete looks at the umpire as if they're being asked a question by an alien life form, you can tell that not enough umpires are checking sticks prior to games.

I suggest umpires check sticks from both teams as they observe the athletes during warm-ups. Check any sticks that are taped up and one or two 'brand new' sticks. During the 2002-03 school year, umpires near where I most often officiated found two brand new sticks without tape on them that did not pass through the ring. I was able to verify this first hand by trying to pass one of these sticks through my stick ring. Sticks that are not manufactured correctly should be able to be returned to the vendor for a full refund; however, whether or not they can be is not an umpire's concern. Such a stick cannot be used.

QUESTION: **Why should the umpire always check about the same number of sticks from both teams?**

ANSWER: **To demonstrate that they are being fair.**

If an umpire has the teams line up before a game to check the sticks, he or she should tell the athletes to have with them any stick that might be used in the game. The stick(s) should be held next to their body (kids play with sticks and will accidentally clunk you in the head) with the handle down. Sticks should be disqualified if they would cause skin injuries due sharp edges, splinters, etc., and if they do not fit through the stick ring. If an umpire disqualifies a stick, it has to be taken it from the athlete and left at the scorer's table. It must remain there until it is fixed/being fixed or the game has ended.

NOTE: Sometimes a stick doesn't pass through the stick ring because the athlete has too much tape wrapped around the stick. The athlete (their coach, their mom, whomever) can try to remove enough tape for it to fit through the stick ring. As soon as a stick is made legal it can be used in the game.

UNIFORM
All field players must be dressed uniformly. The uniform helps umpires and players discern who is playing for which team.

[NFHS (1.5.1.c): NFHS rules are quite specific regarding shirts, socks, and even undergarments. The NFHS rules do NOT say that all players on a team must wear kilts if other members of the team are wearing kilts (or shorts for that matter). In fact, the rules state, "Multiple styles of uniform bottoms may be worn by teammates and may include: shorts, skirts, kilts or pants provided the shin guards are visible." This needs to be emphasized because if a boy were playing on a team that is otherwise made up of girls who are all wearing kilts, he does NOT have to wear a kilt. He could, for example, wear shorts made from somewhat similar material as the material used to make the kilts. By rule, the uniform bottoms only need to be of like color. In short (no pun intended), different uniform bottom styles do not hinder any reasonable umpire or opponent from determining which team the player is on. Also, players and coaches will ask umpires if it is okay for players to wear 'this' or 'that' piece of clothing (a turtleneck, a pair of sweats, long underwear, compression shorts, etc.)? This is especially likely if the game is in a region that gets colder as the hockey season progresses. The answer is to A, check the rule book and B, make it fair. Will the clothing in question make it confusing for the umpires or the opponents to determine which team a player is on? If not, it is probably okay. If the umpires can make this determination without issue, it is no longer an issue impacting the playing of the game—no team is being disadvantaged so there is no penalty. If a coach is still insistent that some rule about clothing is being violated, the umpires should advise him/her to take the issue up with the team's conference or league BUT if the umpires feel the clothing will not create confusion, THE GAME SHALL BE PLAYED. The NFHS rules provide details on how to answer virtually every clothing question one might encounter during high school games (see NFHS rule book for the answers).]

Copyright © 2018 Red Land Youth Field Hockey – Illustration by Kevin McCoy

The fierce-looking teammates illustrated above are uniformly dressed and their uniforms meet the very detailed requirements of NFHS rule 1.5 "Player Uniform". As far as equipment goes, they would need to be wearing shin guards, and mouth guards to play in an NFHS game.

Even though there are differences in the uniform tops and bottoms, they can compete for the same team, in the same game, at the same time.

No umpire or player in any game would be confused wondering for which team these players are competing. The opponents would not be disadvantaged. Therefore, players wearing uniforms like those in the illustration are not violating NFHS rules.

SPECIAL EQUIPMENT: Mouth guards, Shin guards, Masks, Gloves

In addition to the stick, a hockey athlete's main piece of equipment, athletes often use (and are sometimes required to use) mouth guards, shin guards, gloves, and masks. Of course, athlete's playing goalkeeper can wear kickers, leggings, a helmet, face mask, chest protector, throat protector, and various and sundry other padding on their body. Please check the rule book for the rules governing the various types of special equipment.

[NFHS (1.6.1, 1.6.2, 1.6.5): Players must wear shin guards and their shins must be protected from the ankle to just below the knee ("sock guards" can't be worn rolled down). Players must also wear a mouth guard that fits between the athlete's teeth (including molars). On July 3, 2020, the NFHS announced that it reversed a 2010 requirement that players had to wear eye protection. That goggles are now optional is reflected in the NFHS's 2021 rules book.]

NOTE: *Players who replace mouth guards at the game will most likely grab one from the athletic trainer. These mouth guards will typically have a 'football tab' that protrudes from the mouth and attaches the mouth guard to a football helmet's facemask. The protrusion is illegal for all but goalkeepers who may attach the protrusion on their mask.*

QUESTION: **What does an umpire do when an athlete isn't wearing a mouth guard?**

ANSWER: **Without stopping time, direct the athlete to leave the game to get a mouth guard.**

Special Notes

- Big, strong athlete? Legal, a player should not be penalized for his or her size or power

- Reverse stick sweep? Legal, it should not be penalized unless the swing causes actual danger

- Drag flick? Legal, except on Penalty Strokes. This skill should not be penalized for the speed it imparts to ball … it is supposed to be fast!

The Goalkeeper

Did you know that the field hockey swing is the fastest in all of sport? Male hockey players at the Olympic level can hit the ball faster than 100-miles-per hour. As you can imagine, in order to stay alive goalkeepers are protected with some very special equipment. The goalkeeper is also given some very special privileges, unlike those given to any other player. For example, when the goalkeeper is inside his or her circle, any part of his or her body can be used to stop or deflect the ball. The goalkeeper may also use his or her legs and feet to propel the ball. Like all the other players in the competition, the goalkeeper may also use the flat side of the stick to play the ball. And, the goalkeeper can also use their non-stick hand to move the ball in a close-control manner. A goalkeeper can only go as far away from their goal as the 23-meter line (unless they are their team's attacker on a Penalty Stroke).

IMPORTANT: Goalkeepers lose all their special privileges as soon as they leave the circle. In fact, goalkeepers lose all their special privileges as soon as ANY PART OF THEM leaves the circle!

QUESTION: **An aerial is coming towards the circle. It lands a few yards outside and starts bouncing. The goalkeeper is rushing out, she plants one foot inside the circle and kicks the ball away before the ball enters the circle. So, the goalkeeper has one foot on the ground inside the circle and the other foot is off the ground outside the circle when she kicks the ball. The ball is outside the circle. What's the call? Is it a Penalty Corner for an intentional breach inside the attacking 23 meter area or a Penalty Stroke for intentionally breaking the rules inside the circle?**

ANSWER: **A Penalty Corner should be awarded to the attack. The answer to this question highlights how breaches are considered in the context of where the illegal play was made, not where the athlete was when they made the illegal play. The goalkeeper's illegal kick took place outside the circle, in the attacking 23 meter area. Umpires penalize the defense by giving the attack a Penalty Corner when the defense breaks the rules inside the attacking 23.**

STICK

The width of a goalkeeper's stick is so important to his or her ability to stop a shot that umpires should check all goalkeeper sticks prior to the start of a competition. The goalkeeper's stick is usually very lightweight. Though often they are oddly shaped, the goalkeeper's stick(s) must also pass through the same stick ring used to check sticks carried by field players.

NOTE: *Curvy sticks are popular with goalkeepers (and legal for field players). These sticks must also pass through the stick ring but should not be penalized if the outer rim of the umpire's stick ring is too broad to make 'nook and cranny' turns as the stick is passed through an approved ring.*

UNIFORM

The color of goalkeeper's shirt must differ in color from those of his or her teammates and the shirts worn by the field players on the opposing team. To be clear, a goalkeeper from one team can be wearing a shirt that matches the color of the shirt worn by the goalkeeper from the opposing team. The shirt must be on top of any upper-body protection. Be sure to notice during goalkeeper substitutions that the replacement goalkeeper is wearing a legal shirt.

QUESTION: **What does the umpire do when the goalkeeper who has just come into the game is wearing a shirt with a number that matches the goalkeeper's from the other team?**

ANSWER: **That's supposed to be a trick question. Regardless of their position, athletes can have numbers**

that happen to match the number of one of their opponents.

SPECIAL EQUIPMENT: Helmet, Leg Guards, Kickers, Chest Protector, Throat Protector

Goalkeepers must wear protective headgear, leg guards, and kickers. In NCAA and NFHS games, they must also wear chest and throat protection!

[NFHS (1.5.1.a-h): Each team is required to have a fully kitted goalkeeper in the game at all times. The kit includes helmet, fixed facemask, neck collar (called a throat protector), hand protectors, leg guards, kickers, chest protector, and mouth guard. A goalkeeper's mouth guard is allowed to have a protrusion from the mouth. Such a protrusion is not allowed on field players.]

NOTE: *All goalkeepers, no matter what rules, can remove their headgear and any hand protectors when attacking on a Penalty Stroke. All goalkeepers and players with goalkeeping privileges, no matter what rules they're playing under, must wear protective headgear when defending a Penalty Corner or Penalty Stroke. In the Rules of Hockey and the NCAA modifications, a non-goalkeeper can defend Penalty Corners and Penalty Strokes but they must only use their stick to stop the shot. At all levels, any and all players defending a Penalty Stroke must wear a helmet.*

SPECIAL PRIVILEGES

When within 16 yards of the goal they are defending, i.e. when they're in the circle, goalkeepers may:

- Use the whole of their body—front, sides, hands, feet, back, head, etc.—and their stick to stop or deflect the ball

- Use their leg guards, kickers, non-stick hand, and the flat side of their stick to propel the ball

QUESTION: **The goalkeeper accidentally drops his or her hand protector during circle play. As the play continues, an attacker's shot hits the goalkeeper's protector and the ball deflects over the back-line instead of crossing the goal-line. What should the umpire's signal be?**

ANSWER: **The umpire signals for the defense to restart play with what is commonly called a '16', a reference to the maximum number of yards from the back-line that the defense can restart play. The ball was last touched by an attacker. When the hand protector fell off <u>accidentally</u> it became, for the purposes of this discussion, just another blade of grass on the competition surface.**

SPECIAL LIMITATIONS

Goalkeepers must stay in their own defending quarter of the competition surface, unless attacking on a Penalty Stroke.

Special Notes

One should note that the goalkeeper is allowed to play in a manner supported by the way they are required to dress and opponents should not be allowed to take actions against a goalkeeper just because the goalkeeper is wearing protective equipment. For example an attacker may not strike a goalkeeper's legs with his/her stick any more so than they're allowed to whack at the shin pads of a field player. Nor may attackers lean into a goalkeeper or impede the goalkeeper from reaching the ball (obstruction). Further, umpires should not penalize goalkeepers for being goalkeepers.

NOTE: During circle play, especially just before an attacker is going to shoot on a Penalty Corner, umpires should look to see if any attackers are obstructing or physically interfering with the goalkeeper.

Here are some more examples of what to keep in mind in situations involving a goalkeeper:

• Split Save: When the goalkeeper goes down in the performance of split or half-split, sometimes the goalkeeper is a fraction of a second late and ends up 'sitting' on the ball. This is typically very painful and the goalkeeper moves off the ball as fast as he or she can! In the previous century (and by umpires calling the game as if it was being played in the last century), this resulted in a Penalty Stroke. Modern umpires no longer call this a Penalty Stroke. If the goalkeeper accidentally covers the ball and gets off the ball and IF there is an attacker within playing distance, the proper call would be a Penalty Corner. Too often this relatively minor infraction is treated as a major breach and a Penalty Stroke is awarded. That said, if the goalkeeper remains on the ball so that an attacker cannot take a shot, THAT is a Penalty Stroke.

> Similarly, if a goalkeeper jumps on the ball in order to cover it up to prevent an attacker from getting to the ball—or bumps/pushes an attacker away so the attacker cannot play the ball—those are major breaches and offer good cause for awarding a Penalty Stroke!

- Punch Clear: A kick of the ball with no follow through is called a punch clear. If the ball suddenly rises from a punch clear the umpire must decide if the ball was sent airborne as a result of a poorly executed kick or outside influence (a bumpy field or opponent's stick).

- Back of Stick: Like every other player on the field, the goalkeeper may NOT use the back of his or her stick. Watch for this when the goalkeeper is down on his or her knees and the ball is in play in front of the goal. Sometimes it happens on a full 'back-handed' swing at the ball. Sometimes when the attacker pulls the ball across to the left side of the goalkeeper the goalkeeper will reach out and 'poke' the ball away with the back of his or her stick. These are intentional actions and Penalty Stroke worthy.

- New Skills: The modern goalkeeper may stop and deflect a ball with his or her hand(s) and may also play the ball with his or her 'non-stick' hand.

UMPIRES: Be careful that shots deflected away by the goalkeeper don't hit you!

The Captain

Each team must have a captain and the captain must wear a band or other marking indicating their role. The captains are the umpire's biggest resource in managing the behavior of the players and the non-participating team members (coaches and substitutes). The captain is responsible for the conduct of his or her teammates.

[NFHS/NCAA: In NFHS and NCAA games, the head coach is responsible for players on the bench and team staff. In the *Rules of Hockey*, the captain is responsible for everyone, including the coaches.]

Umpires benefit by establishing a collaborative working relationship with the captains from both teams. The key words there are collaborative working relationship. The captains and the umpires work together to establish and maintain the best possible competitive environment for everyone involved. Without help from each team's captain, the umpires are limited in their approach to game management.

 UMPIRES: You work with the captains; captains work with their coach. Remind captains during the pre-game meeting that questions coaches have regarding calls or rules should come to you through the captain. Enforce this expectation during the game. If a coach approaches you directly with a question it is best to say, "Please send your questions through your captain."

Some coaches and umpires have suggested to me that youngsters are not mature enough to perform the duties of being a captain, recommending that the umpires deal more directly with the coaches. This would require that the umpire's focus would have competing interests—the game and the bench. The focus of the umpire should be on the competition and the competitors IN THE GAME. It only makes sense. Suggesting that the umpires' focus should be divided between the competitors and the coaches is simply not supportable.

Utilizing captains is not only what is expected by the rules, it is also an important means of developing the maturity and leadership skills of the captains.

The Team Coach

The job of the coach is to prepare the players for the game. Prepare, as in **before** the game begins.

Although each team typically has a coach, the word 'coach' does not (currently) appear in the *Rules of Hockey* nor does any word that would serve as its surrogate.

Coaches may coach the players but do not enjoy the additional privilege of coaching the umpires.

A coach is not allowed to provide the athletes with continuous excessive coaching. Details and examples of this later but, basically, if a coach's coaching interferes with the game, especially if it delays play or directs players like pulling strings on puppets, that is excessive coaching.

A coach is not allowed to be closer than 5 meters to the sideline. The space next to the sidelines is reserved for the umpires. I call this area outside the lines the officiating space to help communicate to everyone involved who does and does not belong in the space just beyond the sidelines. Coaches, parents, photographers who stand or move about in the officiating space will more than likely end up interfering with an umpire's movement or line-of-sight at a most critical moment. It is imperative that umpires take corrective action when they see someone who doesn't belong in the officiating space. They should take this action when it doesn't seem to even matter so, when it does matter, it won't be too late!

NOTE: I recommend that coaches who want to pace back and forth, do so behind their team's bench – as in ice hockey. In this way, they won't accidentally move into the officiating space and, especially for younger age groups, members of the team who are on the bench will hear whatever instructions the coach feels compelled to give to the players in the game.

Umpires do not have x-ray vision nor do they have radar. Good umpires are typically moving in a direction they are not looking. They move parallel to sidelines looking into the game – almost never watching where they're going. They do this to maintain an optimum view of the play so they can make appropriate calls. Coaches who haven't had many mobile umpires may not realize that the officiating space is actually needed by the umpires.

 UMPIRES: Ensure before the game starts that the officiating space is clear of stick bags, water bottles, hockey balls, etc. This includes the officiating space beyond the back-lines on the near side of the goal (goalkeepers often need a water bottle with them; it should be on the side of the goal to the goalkeeper's right).

QUESTION: **What does an umpire do when a coach is in the umpire's officiating space?**

ANSWER: **In the *Rules of Hockey*, the team's captain**

should be cautioned and warned, i.e. carded, for subsequent violations. In games governed by the NFHS and NCAA modifications, the head coach is be carded.

You know a game was well coached when the game is over and no one remembers seeing either coach.

[NFHS (1.9): Each team must have at least one coach.]

The Fans

Bleachers crowded with wildly enthusiastic fans can enhance the game experience for all concerned. In some countries, the fans create so much noise that the U.S. national teams have played in gyms with music blaring in an attempt to simulate the roaring crowds they'll find at international venues. A problem for the fans in the USA, however, is that extremely few know any of the rules. Even parents who played hockey when they were younger don't realize the degree to which so much has changed in the sport they fondly remember. In this country, I have seen umpires 'shut down' enthusiastic fans, I suppose because it is such a rare occasion to have fans, let alone rowdy fans. I ask these umpires to think about how taking such actions would play out at an NFL stadium. Fans are typically the domain of site personnel (if no one else is available that means the home team's head coach) and only become an umpire's concern if the fan is disrupting the game.

The Umpires

The more you learn about the rules of field hockey and how umpires are taught to umpire a game, the more you'll understand field hockey.

Each game is officiated by two umpires who partner with each other and work with the captains to ensure that every contest, and each competition within a game, is fair.

For any given situation, one of the umpires is the "responsible umpire" based on the location and/or direction of the play (more on this later). The responsible umpire works with the "other umpire" in a partnership that is most often subtle but sometimes overt (meaning that sometimes you won't see the umpires working with each other to sort something out and other times you'll see the responsible umpire make an obvious inquiry of the other umpire regarding a play).

Why would one umpire ever need help from their partner? Simple, the ball is small and, in comparison, the bodies of the players are huge! When one umpire's vision of the play is blocked he or she quickly looks to his or her partner for help in making a call or to see that no call needs to be made.

There will be times that an umpire will find himself or herself playing the caboose at the end of a long "train" of players—the ball is the engine—and the umpire hasn't a prayer of seeing the ball (see example in the photo below). When this happens to an umpire, they can look for help from the other umpire. The umpires know when their partner is most likely to need help and should be in a position and prepared to help—like when one umpire sees that his or her partner is at the end of the train!

Photograph by Ramon Gibert

In order to officiate, the umpire has special tools that he or she can use in the execution of his or her duties. The primary tool, after having a complete knowledge of the rules, is a whistle. The umpire uses the whistle to talk to the players. Of course, cards help the umpire manage the game. However, it is the umpire's fitness, positioning, coursework, concentration, understanding, demeanor, philosophy, relationship skills, experience, posture, signals, style, and other personal attributes that separate successful umpires from underperformers.

Umpires are not just impartial judges of the game. They are courageous human beings, nourished by the significant challenges each and every minute of any game can bring.

A friend of mine who coaches field hockey, Heather Serverson, said, *"Rather than 'enforcers of the rules', field hockey umpires should think of themselves, and perhaps be known as, flow facilitators."*

I think she has it right.

ACCOUTREMENTS

Uniform | Cards | Stick Ring | Radios | Recording Materials |
Visor | Coin | Rulebook | Whistles | Water | Sunblock

UNIFORM

Umpires are professionals and need to look the part! Their uniform should be in very good condition. Wrinkle free might be impossible but, that's the target. If their shirt is faded or torn, it should be replaced. Ideally, the umpires should be dressed EXACTLY the same, allowing only gender specific differences (kilts for girls and women, slacks for boys and men).

Shirts must match in color and, whenever possible, in style.

At the highest levels, female umpires always wear a kilt. In some settings shorts or full-length slacks are permissible but, kilts are far and away the choice for female hockey umpires. Black knee socks are also the norm, even if it's nice tanning weather.

Male umpires should wear full-length slacks. At the highest levels, male umpires always wear slacks. In some settings shorts are permissible but, slacks are far and away the choice for male hockey umpires.

Wearing pants? Never wear sweat pants. Performance slacks are readily available. Slacks/kilts should be black.

Umpires should wear shoes/cleats that are do not distract the players from the ball. I have seen umpires wear white sneakers. The hockey ball is white (typically). One never wants to introduce an article of clothing, especially one worn near the ground, which a player might mistake for the ball.

UMPIRES: Please, when you're officiating, it is NOT the time to concern yourself with tan lines. Do NOT roll up your sleeves or otherwise 'contort' your uniform. Do NOT wear compression shorts/pants, bike shorts/pants, or spandex shorts or pants as your outer layer of clothing. If you're wearing them as an undergarment, make sure they remain completely OUT OF VIEW!

RULEBOOK

Umpires must make sure they not only have a print-out of the current *Rules of Hockey* but also any applicable modifications, tiebreaker instructions, and interpretation instructions from their umpire organization or national association.

COIN

A coin is needed to toss at the beginning of the game and for overtime periods (if played).

WHISTLE

Do NOT get a whistle that has a little ball on the inside (if the ball gets stuck, the whistle won't work). The FOX 40 Classic is my recommendation for a main outdoor whistle. The secondary whistle should be what is commonly referred to as a 'train whistle.' I've seen it advertised as a 'tweeter' but it should be called a 'tooter' because, in my opinion, the sound it makes is more like a toot than a tweet. A tooter is used during tournament play where multiple games are often being played very close together (one game is officiated using a 'tooter' and the one next to it is officiated using a Classic).

Umpires should have a second set of whistles in case one set is dropped in the mud.

You should, whenever possible, go out of your way to match the whistle that your partner is using. This is done for the benefit of the players, so that both umpires sound the same— like a team!

NOTE: Metal whistles get rather cold during cold weather games and they're tough on the teeth.

CARDS

Umpires must have cards (green, yellow, and red). You might think that goes without saying but, unfortunately, it must be said. Some older umpires will brag (think they're bragging), *"I've never had to use cards so I don't carry them."* This is an umpire who doesn't have an understanding of the modern game. They probably also blow their whistle when play is in their partner's circle and make goal scorers carry the ball out to the center-line.

Cards are specifically designed for hockey (a green triangle, a yellow square, and a red circle). They should be carried out-of-view, in a pocket. Umpires will be running up and down the competition surface—we don't want to see their cards flapping around like the mating plumage of a rare tropical bird.

 UMPIRES: The cards are different shapes so you can feel their shape before taking the correct card from your pocket. Another reason is that many men are colorblind so the different shapes help everyone quickly identify the severity of the penalty.

RECORDING MATERIALS

The *Rules of Hockey* REQUIRE that umpires have materials to record goals and cards. I emphasize this because many old-minded umpires don't do a good job of recording game events and might tell new umpires not to bother, claiming that keeping score is not an umpire's job. Therefore, not keeping score or recording cards would be considered umpire misconduct.

Of late I've noticed a number of hockey umpires using a small 'tumbler' to keep the score of the game. This is insufficient to meet the requirement as stated in the rules because it only keeps the score of the game and no record of cards. Further, using such a device doesn't provide more veracity about the outcome the umpire is reporting than pulling the score from memory.

How can the umpire demonstrate that they remembered to turn the tumbler each time a team scored? What evidence does the umpire have that they turned the correct side of the tumbler when the Red team scored as opposed to the Blue team?

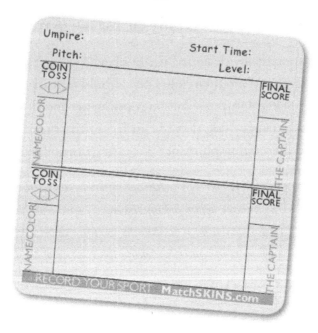

Illustration of yellow card with transparent, erasable, reusable "skin" in place. They stick like a strong PostIt®, last for about 10 games, peel off, and can be written on even in the rain. Available at MatchSKINS.com.

A written record carries with it an authenticity with which it is difficult to quarrel.

A properly trained umpire keeps a thorough and accurate record of game events during each competition. In the old days it was thought to be satisfactory to simply keep score by writing slashes on the palm of your hand. The umpire and the game are best served by having a record of each goal scored, how the goal was scored (field goal, Penalty Corner, or Penalty Stroke), the number of the player who scored, the team that scored (Red, White, or Blue in the example games above), and, at a minimum, in which period the goal was scored.

Demonstrating in what sequence the goals were scored is even better and can be achieved by noting the time of each goal. If ever challenged about the score or other details about the game, the umpire simply refers to his or her MatchSKIN™ (or similarly substantive recording material).

Does having this kind of record keeping actually matter?

At USA Field Hockey's 2006 Women's National Indoor Tournament, a game I just finished officiating was listed by the scorekeeper at the table as having an outcome of 4-1 (a goal differential of 3). I had details for each goal and a final score of 5-1. I asked the other umpire what score she had. She looked at the scorer's table and said, *"Four to one."* Still concerned, I asked the captains and they looked at the scorer's table and one said, *"Four to one,"* and the other nodded in agreement. I was happy to be wrong but because goal differentials were being taken into account to determine final standings in the tournament, having an accurate score could prove crucial in the final outcome of the entire tournament so, I asked each captain to meet with her team and tally the goals each player claimed to have scored.

When the captains came back with a total of 5-1, which was exactly what I had on my card. I doubt that if all I had was a tumbler or slash marks on my hand that the final outcome would have been corrected.

STICK RING

All sticks must be able to pass through an approved stick ring with a 51mm / 2 inch internal opening. A ring made out of PVC piping or other bendable material should not be used. Umpires are expected to have a ring for this stick check.

[NCAA: The NCAA recommends that sticks be checked at least 45 minutes before the game.]

RADIOS

Most high performance umpires are wearing 'open mic' radios (not walkie talkies) to improve game management by enhancing their communications with each other. Walkie talkies have fallen out of favor with umpires, despite their low cost. Reasons include the need to fumble with a walkie talkie's push-to-talk button, extra noises (start and finish beeps, static), and the unsecure nature of walkie talkie communications (scanners can make their use impossible).

Umpiring radios are available for sale on BolsterHockey.com.

VISOR/CAP

When officiating, umpires need to see the game, make eye contact with players and their officiating partner. They shouldn't put anything between their eyes and the game that is DESIGNED TO REDUCE visual information!

If umpires have to protect their eyes from the sun, they can wear a visor/cap, they should NOT wear dark or mirrored sunglasses. And, if umpires are wearing eyeglasses for vision correction, they should be wearing tinted contact lenses or glasses with lenses that don't darken significantly in sunlight. Umpires should never wear glasses with dark or mirrored lenses.

 UMPIRES: If medical reasons require you to wear sunglasses with dark lenses that hide your eyes, then at least take them off when speaking with your officiating partner, coaches, and team captains (for example during the pre-game meeting, between periods, and other discussions).

WATER

Protecting oneself from dehydration and dehydration related injuries, like muscle cramps, is just as important for umpires as it is for the players. Umpires should bring with them to every game a personal water supply.

SUNBLOCK

Skin cancer is a real threat to players, coaches, and umpires. Wearing sunblock helps ensure healthy skin.

CHAPTER 2

UMPIRING AS A WINDOW

If you're new to hockey you'll learn from watching that safety is a major factor governing the game. In fact, the rules of the game are such that male and female athletes of many different physiques can compete safely with and against each other.

Given the combative nature of hockey competitions, umpires are needed to apply the rules without bias for or against either team. Good umpires provide a playing environment that allows the athletes to reach their full potential. Umpires also have to immediately penalize dangerous play that competitors sometimes resort to in the heat of battle.

NOTE: The presence of umpires does NOT alleviate the responsibility that coaches and players have in keeping the game safe. In fact, safety is each player's responsibility. The umpires can only penalize unsafe play when they see, they can't prevent it.

Umpires are asked, as part of their responsibilities, to 'protect' skill. Here is an example of how an umpire protects skill:

If an attacker for the Red team is dribbling happily up the side-line and a Blue team defender crashes in and the ball pops out of bounds and the umpire is not sure who touched the ball last—the umpire is advised to give the ball back to the attacker who had skillful possession.

The point is, if the defender had not so unskillfully tackled the attacker who was skillfully dribbling, the ball wouldn't be out of bounds. It would still be in the possession of the Red team.

QUESTION: **If the Red player is dribbling up the side-line and a Blue team defender crashes in and the ball pops out of bounds and the Blue player makes disruptive contact with the Red player's body, what should the umpire do?**

ANSWER: **Award possession to the Red team and card the Blue team player.**

Here are some additional 'big picture' officiating tips for umpires (that everyone should know):

- Be consistent. The call umpires make in the first five minutes of a game should be the same made in the last five seconds of double-overtime. Umpires should look harder early in the game for violations that can help establish their consistency. If an umpire knows he or she is picky about coaches being outside the team area late in the game, they should be picky about it early on.

- Be fair and look fair. Is the umpire in position to make a call? I call it the 50-50-50 rule. If it's a 50-50 call, and the umpire is 50 meters away...don't make the call! If the play is right under the other umpires' nose...don't make the call from the other side-line!

 UMPIRES: Actually, you should NEVER make ANY 50-50 call unless it involves danger. If you're not sure if there was an obstruction, but you think there might have been, don't make a call. If you're not sure if when a player kicked the ball it was to his or her advantage, don't call it. On the other hand, ALWAYS make a 50-50 call that involves danger. If you're thinking that MAYBE a player's contact with an opponent was dangerous, call it and card it!

- Be in position/look composed. Get to the right distance and be at the correct angle. You don't want to be at the end of the train where the ball is the locomotive, the players are the passenger cars, and you're the caboose! Of course, sometimes it happens and it is completely unavoidable. You have to "sprint" a yard or two in one direction or another just to get the correct angle. You'll hear coaches telling players to, *"Move your feet."* Umpires should move theirs too and try to avoid constantly jumping and squatting and leaning and, generally, looking jittery but, umpires should do whatever they have to in order to make the best possible call. We don't want umpires to look like they're walking on hot coals, nor do we want umpires looking like they're in a state of sedation.

- Be fit. The game is faster than ever. Being fit is fair to the competitors, who work so hard getting ready to do their job. Is it fair if umpires are not ready to match the competitors efforts during competitions? Of course not. Umpires need to be athletes!

- Establish management details early. Although umpires don't want to focus on minutiae, they do have to pay attention to details, especially early in the game (first 5 to 10 minutes). Don't let 5 meters mean 4½ meters! In NFHS games, 5 yards is already fewer than 5 meters so don't let 5 yards slip to only 3 or 4 yards.

- Communicate, facilitate play, encourage an open, flowing game, communicate – be a flow facilitator. Don't jump to penalize small mishaps (inconsequential ball contact with the foot is minutiae). Don't make players work through fouls. If they have to fight through a foul, they probably need the umpire's whistle. Tell the players to "play on" when they have the advantage (when you won't be blowing your whistle). Use a normal speaking voice to tell the players to, for example, *"Watch your stick. Keep your tackle clean."* when they're going in for what might be a rough tackle. That tells the players what to expect if they screw up the tackle and tells them that the umpire is hoping for a good outcome. When the ball does make inconsequential contact with their foot or the back of the stick and the umpire is not going to call it as a foul, using a normal speaking voice to say, *"Try not to let the ball hit your foot like that,"* tells the players around you that you saw it, considered it, and judged it to be incidental.

- Be firm. Umpires don't have to be mean to mean business. Umpires don't have to point a finger or scowl, they just have to let the athletes know early, perhaps with a chest-out, stomach-in, shoulders-back posture, a hard whistle, and strong arm signals that the umpire means business.

- Stay ahead of the complaints. Umpires should loudly say, *"Play on!"* when they judge what looked like a foul not to be one! They should say, *"No danger, play on!"* just as loudly when they know people (coaches and fans) with a different perspective on the play might think what just happened was dangerous.

- Communicate with partner. Even when using wireless communication devices, umpires should make eye contact with each other during stoppages in play, not just when they're in trouble. Demonstrate that communication with a nod in agreement, a thumb up for a righteous call, etc. (Don't demonstrate disagreement!)

- Predict the future. Umpires will thrive by considering what might happen next. Coaches are constantly asking their players to, *"Look up!"* That's a good lesson for umpires. Umpires should just stare at the ball—they shouldn't "ball watch." Umpires should raise their head and look around. The play at the ball is happening NOW. Umpires need to constantly prepare for what is going to happen NEXT! What will the players try to do? In a given situation, umpires need to anticipate what the players will try to do. What tactics might they employ? What skills might they use? What foul might they be tempted to commit? Will the defender closing from behind hack the attacker who is about to enter the circle? The umpire should be preparing to call a Penalty Corner or anticipating that they'll have to call a Penalty Stroke – and hoping that they don't have to. If the defender does hack the attacker as predicted, the umpire should be equally ready to hold for advantage, to see if the attacker can work through the foul and take a shot on goal. Don't put the brakes on the game just because of what the defender is trying to!

- Be a student of the game. What are the new skills that are being introduced to field players and goalkeepers? Will they be employed this year? A lot, a little?

Usually umpires blow the whistle to say, *"No,"* and, then, award possession of the ball to the other team. Every so often umpires get to blow the whistle to say *"Yes,"* because a goal has been scored (or the attack can begin a Penalty Corner, Penalty Stroke, or a Shoot Out).

[NFHS (10.2): NFHS umpires don't have to whistle to begin a Penalty Corner.]

Chances are that umpires will most often blow the whistle because:

1. An athlete has played the ball to his or her team's advantage with something other than the flat side of his or her stick (advancing). For example, a mid-fielder that kicks the ball ahead to his or her teammate.

NOTE: It is NOT a foul just because the ball makes contact with a player's foot. First, the 'kicker' must gain an advantage from the contact. Second, if one player kicks the ball forward but the ball is "picked up" by the other team, the umpire should NOT blow his or her whistle because the other team already has possession (unless a Penalty Corner or Penalty Stroke is in order).

HINT: Let's say a Blue team member in a girl's game has been sent the ball with a hard pass. The receiver plays the ball with her stick and THEN it happens to knock off her foot. Unless there is someone near her or she's in the circle and this foot contact helps her to take a shot or clear the ball away, chances are there is NO WAY this is a foul. In fact, when the ball hit her foot it probably slowed down her ability to do whatever she was hoping to do when she got the ball. This, if anything, created a disadvantage for her team by allowing the opposing team time to react. Same player, same pass but this time she stops the hard pass with her foot and THEN plays the ball with their stick. Sorry, that's too much like soccer, eh, football.

QUESTION: **If the Blue teams sends a hard pass off the mark and it is traveling with speed to a red player standing all by himself by the side-line, and the ball makes contact with the red player's body preventing it from traveling out of bounds, what should the umpire do?**

ANSWER: **As long as the body contact wasn't intentional, say, *"Play on."* When a rule is broken, the umpire only needs to penalize it when the opponent has been disadvantaged by the breach. In this case, had the ball traveled out of bounds without contacting the red player's body, possession would have gone to the Red team from the side-line. Now, the Red team has possession near the side-line.**

2. The ball has been played in a dangerous manner or in a manner that might lead to dangerous play (danger). For example, an aerial might have been put into the air without any danger to anyone BUT as the ball travels back to earth it lands in the middle of a large group of

players right in front of the goal. The whistle is blown because the ball was played in a manner that could become dangerous as it returns to the ground. The same aerial to a place free of opponents would, obviously, not be considered dangerous. If an opponent runs into the space where the passer's teammate is waiting for the ball to come down, now it is the opponent that is creating the potential danger. Similarly, if one of the passer's teammates runs into the space where the passer's opponent is waiting for the ball to come down, now it is the team that started the aerial that is creating the potential danger.

NOTE: *When an aerial goes up safely we have a "falling ball" and when there is a falling ball we look for what I call the "None or One" status of the place in which the ball will fall. If there is nobody there, play on. If there is one person there, play on and continue to judge that the ball is played in a safe manner as it returns to the competition surface. If there are players from both teams there, now you have to judge the play with more sophistication. If the teammate of the lifter is not leaving the space (giving 5 meters to the opponent) whistle and give possession to the opponents where the ball was lifted.*

3. The player with the ball blocks an opponent from reaching the ball (obstruction). The attacker can dribble around in circles, dribble through his or her legs, spin/turn and dribble away, but he or she cannot place his or her body between the defender and a reachable ball. Think of how a basketball player would typically use his or her body to protect the ball from an opponent by dribbling backwards into the defender while keeping the ball away from the defender. That is

not allowed in hockey and is called obstruction. Still, even a behind the back pass is allowed in hockey if it is done quickly enough that the defender could not have reached and was not attempting to reach the ball at the moment it was behind the attacker's back.

NOTE: A player has an obligation to legally approach the ball. He may not run through an opponent to reach the ball.

4. A teammate of the player with possession has moved between the dribbler and a defender and moves to interfere with an opponent's ability to reach what would have otherwise been a reachable ball (obstruction). In basketball this is called a pick. In hockey it's called third-party obstruction and is an 'off the ball' foul. Umpires won't see this foul until they stop watching the ball and, instead, look up and watch the play as a whole. Third-party obstruction is illustrated and discussed in more detail later in this book.

5. An opponent making contact with a goalkeeper. This physical issue isn't, of course, limited to an attacker using his or her body to knock (even ever so gently) the goalkeeper off his or her mark. In fact, a 'professional foul' of using upper body contact in the microsecond before an exaggerated but clean stick action is now part of the game (kind of like a pickpocket bumping into the victim's chest while pulling the wallet from the victim's pants). Use of the body in such a manner is against the rules and should be penalized.

As mentioned above, there will be other times when the umpire blows the whistle to say, *"Yes."* For example, *"Yes, that was a goal,"* and when there is any uncertainty displayed by the players regarding whether the ball has gone out of bounds. In such an instance, umpires blow the whistle three times in rapid succession to get the attention of all the players. They're saying, *"Yes, the ball went out of bounds but, stop playing!"* (If the umpire is close enough to the players they can say, *"It's out. It's out!"* By the same token, if the ball isn't out but is on a line, it is helpful to say, *"Play on. Play on. It's not out."*

There are, basically, only seven things that stop the flow of a hockey game.

- Fouls

- Ball Out of bounds

- Goals

- Timeouts (injuries and video reviews) and End Period (including end of game)

- Misconduct

- Injuries

- Crazy happens (a dog runs away with the ball)

NOTE: Umpires officiate from positions inside and outside of the competition surface. The officiating space extends beyond the competition surface and must be clear of inanimate objects (tripping hazards), coaches, spectators, etc. This "outside" officiating space measures 5 meters beyond the sidelines and back-lines [5 yards in NFHS games].

WHEN AN INJURY HAPPENS

When an athlete is injured, the game is NOT stopped immediately by the umpires unless play is moving toward the injured player or if the player suffered what appears to be a serious head injury. Also, if at the time of the injury, the ball doesn't clear the immediate vicinity of the injured player the umpires should stop the game immediately.

Even if there is no timeout called, the umpire "without the play" must RUN to the injured player (while paying attention to the game action), bend over them and ask, *"Do you need assistance?"* Running to the athlete demonstrates to everyone that the umpire sees that the player is injured. This behavior is not a rule but was introduced as a 'current practice' in 2007.

If the player answers, *"Yes!"* or can't answer or clearly needs medical attention (blood, deformity, etc.), the umpire watches for the first appropriate opportunity to signal timeout, does so and then signals the medical staff onto the competition surface so the injured player can be given appropriate attention.

When the medical staff is permitted onto the competition

surface, only the medical staff is allowed onto the surface to attend the injured athlete. After the athlete has been visited by medical personal, the umpires will typically allow a coach to come out too. Problems, however, have occurred when parents come out to meet with the athlete. This is a tricky situation as it is very difficult to tell the parents, *"No."* The key to remember is that once the game begins, only players are allowed onto the competition surface without being INVITED by the umpires.

If the player answers, *"No,"* then the umpire says, *"Okay. Get up."* Of course, players are tough but not necessarily smart at these moments. If there is blood or the attending umpire thinks the player ought to be seen by the medical staff, the umpire will call timeout and bring on the medics.

Umpires do NOT otherwise attend to the injured player. In fact, once medical staff is attending to the player, the umpire should move away from the injured athlete and meet with the other umpire. It is not the role of the umpires to help move other players away—that's up to the coach—or direct teams to this or that area of the field. The umpires should instead have a discussion about what happened and, most important, what happens next. How play will restart? The umpires should use this time to make sure they're on the same page so that when the game restarts, it does so smoothly.

RESTARTING PLAY: The injured athlete's team doesn't get the ball just because one of their players was injured. In my experience, more often than not it has been the injured athlete who was playing dangerously (fouled) at the time they were hurt. For example, a defender comes up behind an attacker and runs into the attacker's backswing. Or, a defender reaches in from behind to make a tackle from the left side of the attacker and is hit by a follow through. In these cases, despite the injury to the defender, the ball needs to be awarded to the athlete who lost the chance to properly pass the ball because the defender put him or herself in danger.

What if play must be stopped when a Blue team player is hurt and the Red team is in possession of the ball? A bully restarts play for all 'no foul' circumstances (for example, the ball breaks apart during play).

QUESTION: **Who gets the ball when the attack shoots the ball with 5 seconds to go in the game and this goal would win the state championship BUT on its way to the goal the ball splits into pieces?**

ANSWER: **Whenever the ball breaks apart during play, even during a shot on goal, play restarts with a bully.**

How Does Umpire Partnership Work

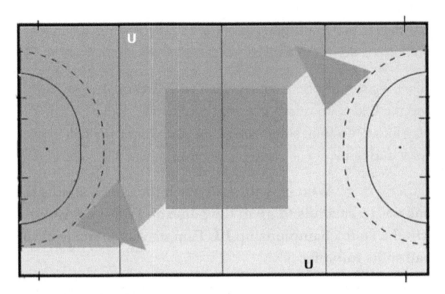

SPLIT RESPONSIBILITIES

Each umpire is 'assigned' half of the competition surface. The surface is split on a diagonal between opposite corners—with a generous bend toward the back-line as the division crosses the 23-meter line. The square in the diagram above illustrates an area of shared responsibility. The triangles are shared based on individual preferences and what's agreed to during the discussions prior to the match.

Generally, the umpires stay on opposite sides of the play, trying to stay within 20 to 25 meters of the other umpire's relative position. Maintaining a near-constant position relative to each other enables the officiating team to quickly find each other during the competition. Imagine that the umpires are connected by an invisible magnetic force that reaches across the competition surface. The graphic above illustrates this division and positions the umpires where they might stand before the competition is started/restarted with a center-pass (though, if the team on the left side of the center-line was starting with the ball, the umpire near the bottom side-line might be even closer to the back-line). While play is in the midfield (between the 23-meter lines), this relative position to each other doesn't change very much regardless of where the play is on the competition surface.

REMINDER: Umpires officiate from positions inside and outside of the competition surface and watch the play, not where they're running. Therefore, the officiating space beyond the boundary lines must be clear of inanimate objects (tripping hazards), coaches, spectators, etc.

At the start of the contest, the umpire near the bottom of the diagram, let's call him Nick, stands near one of the sidelines and faces the center of the competition surface. Nick has responsibility for an increasingly larger portion of the competition surface to his right. This includes, to the complete exclusion of the other umpire's whistle, the entirety of the circle/scoring zone on Nick's right.

As play moves into Nick's end of the competition surface, Nick becomes the responsible umpire (he's the umpire 'with the play'), in the same instant, the other umpire becomes, well, the other umpire. Common labels for these umpires are the lead/managing umpire and the trail/support umpire respectively. In Europe the umpire with the play (the managing umpire) is called the 'engaged' umpire. The problem is, that means that the 'other' umpire (the support umpire) is called the 'disengaged' umpire. It could be a cultural thing but at no time during a hockey game should any umpire of any sport be thought of as being disengaged!

NOTE: Regardless of whether the umpire on the side of the competition surface closest to the team benches is in the lead or trail position, he or she is known as the head umpire. Despite this title, neither umpire has more authority than the other nor does it imply that one umpire has more seniority than the other.

The umpire in the supporting position, let's call her Swati, must watch the play on the ball when it is likely that Nick, the umpire in the lead position, won't be able to see. Specifically, Swati should:

1. Closely watch the play on the ball when the ball is in on the nearside of the circle to her left

2. Swati needs to be ready to give a BIG, clear arm signal (for example Penalty Corner or Penalty Stroke) if and ONLY if Nick asks for help

COACHES AND FANS: Watch the umpire closely during these times to see if you've got a couple of good umpires out there who know how to work with each other.

The other umpire NEVER, NEVER, NEVER blows his or her whistle to make a call when play is in the responsible umpire's circle! In this example, Swati does NOT blow her whistle for breaches that take place in Nick's circle.

PARTNER ETIQUETTE

Here are a short list of Do's and Don'ts umpire teams should follow:

*   Do concentrate on the game even when your partner is the responsible umpire and has the play (unless you think your partner will get blocked out, you should NOT be watching

the ball, look for off-ball 'activities')

- Do be in position when your partner looks for help

- Do be ready to give your partner a clear signal when they look to you for help and make your signal BIG

- Don't, when the play is clearly your partner's to call, show a signal UNLESS your partner clearly looks to you for help (if you're using electronic communication devices, only help when you are asked)

- Do keep your eye on off-ball play in and around your partner's circle (watch for the cheap stuff, the pushing and shoving) especially when the ball is right under your partner's nose

- Do show you're partner a signal, a BIG one, when they look to you or ask for your help

- Don't make a call on a play that is happening right under your partner's nose

- Don't blow your whistle and make calls in your partner's circle

- Don't challenge your partner's calls—at least, not in public—even with your body language

POSITIONING DURING PLAY

If every few seconds a dot representing each umpire's position were placed on a diagram of a competition surface, the "J" patterns illustrated on the graphic would likely emerge.

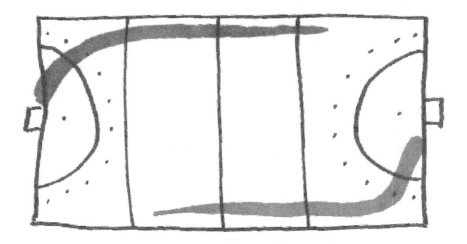

The exact positions that each umpire must take up during any given moment of the game will be dictated by movement of play and the location of players—and umpires will absolutely use the officiating space outside the sidelines and back-lines.

The umpires should always keep the ball on their left and should never cross to the other side of an imaginary line drawn across the middle of the field connecting the goals.

DANGERS UMPIRES HAVE TO WORRY ABOUT

Even though most competition sites are fairly safe, some are dangerous. I have cancelled games due to exposed manhole covers, raised sprinkler heads, and long grass. I've had site personnel use a nearby trash can to cover a two foot tall pipe installed just a few yards beyond the back-line. The pipe was to (eventually) support a new scoreboard but, until it was covered by the trash can, it was an impalement hazard. I've also had site personnel fill in 'career ending' holes. Umpires want to make sure during their warm-up that they investigate areas of the competition surface and the surrounding officiating space where they might need to go. Check outside the lines! For example, check beyond the back-lines and sidelines for holes, depressions, rocks, water pipes, gullies, fallen branches, water bottles, hockey balls (especially dull colored hockey balls), etc.

No one should allow athletes to compete on a site that has dangerous elements that cannot be rectified.

[NFHS: Parents watching games governed by the NFHS can notify the school's state association when a competition surface fails to meet safety and playing standards. If you would like a copy of a field safety report form with state association fax numbers please visit: UmpireHockey.com/safety]

QUESTION: **What do umpires do if they find a bunch of broken glass a few feet away from the back-line?**

ANSWER: **If it can't be cleared away by the facility's ground crew, they do not start the game.**

In addition to the 'dangers' involved with running around officiating any athletic competition, there are a number of dangers that I would like to highlight (in no particular order) for umpires. Getting hit by a stick is the first; getting hit by a ball is the second; colliding with a coach is the third; and, fourth, tripping over something left in front of the benches.

1. Umpires are most likely going to get hit by a stick if the umpire is standing too close to a player who is restarting play from a side-line (particularly a young one who one might feel safe around because of their small size). Please remember that the hockey stick is about three feet long and it is typically held at the end of a person's arms AND younger players tend to miss the ball and swing wildly. When a player on the side-line prepares to hit or follows through on their hit... WATCH OUT!

2. Umpires can be easily get hit by the ball during circle play when a shot deflects up from a field player's stick or the goalkeeper's pads. This can also happen standing on the back-line helping your partner administer a Penalty Stroke (see diagram below).

NOTE: Throughout this book the umpire in the support/trail position is illustrated wearing a cap. The managing umpire is not wearing a cap.

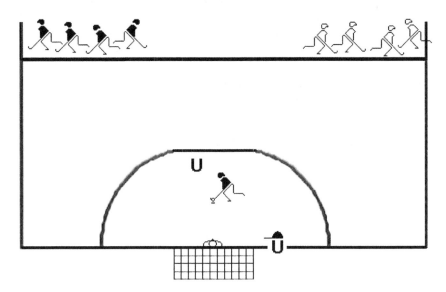

 UMPIRES: On a Penalty Stroke, the umpire on the back-line (the support umpire) ONLY watches to see if the ball crosses the goal-line.

3. The hockey umpire does a lot of running in one direction while looking in another. Sometimes the umpire will even run backwards. In short, umpires are usually not looking where they're going – instead they run fast and focus on the game. The space outside both sidelines must be free of tripping hazards … and coaches! When a coach comes within 5 meters/yards of

the side-line, they have left the coaching area defined in the rulebook and put the umpire in harm's way by putting themselves in the officiating space. Maybe coaches who violate the coaching area boundary should be given only one 'free' reminder and immediately carded on subsequent violations. I strongly recommend an immediate carding. They might ask, *"How about a warning first?"* My answer, *"The rules are the warning."*

 UMPIRES: Trust me, you will find, after years and years of giving verbal warnings or making requests (even when you say, "Please") that the simplest and very best way to modify a coach's behavior is to card the behavior you want changed.

4. If someone sees an umpire coming (but most don't because, like the umpire, they're watching the game), they'll get out of the umpire's way. Sticks, water bottles, stick bags, extra hockey balls, chairs, etc., etc., are not life forms—they won't get out of the way. Umpires must, for their own safety, make sure that the officiating space next to the sidelines and back-lines is clear of all inanimate objects before starting the game.

CHAPTER 3

FAIRNESS VS. SAFETY

Keep the Game Fair

The most important job of every umpire is to keep the game fair. When an umpire makes a huge call just inches away from the goal-line, 50% of the people watching the game will think the greatest umpire on the planet is officiating and an equal number will wonder why the umpire thinks he or she can get away with officiating with his or her eyes closed. Who among all those watching the contest have the responsibility to make the call without prejudice? Only the umpires.

Being fair is every umpire's number one job. Demonstrating fairness is a skill employed by high performance umpires.

When the ball pops out of bounds off of two sticks and the umpire doesn't know which team touched it last, the umpire must instantly pick a direction. And, if the umpire is confronted with the same difficult situation again, he or she must instantly give possession to the OTHER team. That's fair.

An alternative is to give possession to the team defending the half of the field in which the ball crossed the side-line.

If the umpires check to see if the Blue team's goalkeeper has a stick that will fit through the stick ring, they must check the stick that belongs to the other team's goalkeeper too. That's fair.

After the umpires learns the name of the Blue team's captain, they must make sure they learn the name of the other team's captain and demonstrate that they know the names of both captains by using their names during the pregame meeting with the captain. That's fair.

Fairness extends to an umpire's personal conduct on game days and during multi-day tournaments (before, during, and after games). Umpires are likely to run into former coaches, former teammates, players who might be friends with their kids, etc. No matter how well an umpire knows a player or coach or even a fan, or how much the umpire might have missed them since the last time he or she saw that person, the only contact you should have with them on game day or during a multi-day tournament is a professional handshake. Umpires can be friendly and genuine but not overly friendly. Umpires have to remain focused on their professionalism at all times. When an umpire sees someone who he or she suspects might want to give them a big hug, the umpire should be proactive and reach out his or her right hand as they approach so they know well in advance that you'll only be shaking hands with them. I've had people say to me, *"What? No hug?"* I tell them, *"When I'm umpiring I only shake hands."* It is that simple.

Again, it isn't enough to call a fair game; good umpires do things that demonstrate they are fair.

Keep the Game Safe (by penalizing danger)

Safety is NOT the umpire's job—penalizing dangerous play is!

Imagine me teaching new umpires that their job is to keep the game safe. Now, picture that during that umpire's first assignment player #21 is hurt during a rough tackle. If we coach umpires that the safety of the players is the umpire's job, then, clearly, that umpire is a failure because someone got hurt during a game they were officiating. Is that fair? No. It is not fair. It's not even logical.

Safety guides any rules committee in its consideration of what rules should govern play but umpires are NOT responsible for making the game safe. That would be impossible. Only the players can make the game safe. Umpires must take seriously their responsibility to penalize athletes who play dangerously.

It is every competitor's responsibility to play safely and it is every coach's job to teach athletes how to play safely. Umpires, however, are specifically barred from coaching. An umpire's only opportunity to "teach the athletes how to play safely" is by penalizing dangerous play. In fact, it is critical that umpires properly penalize dangerous play.

ACTIVITY: If a player is hit in the face with an opponent's stick, describe a scenario in which the athlete who was injured was the one who played dangerously.

Umpires only fail the "safety test" when they fail to appropriately penalize athletes who play dangerously or are (or appear to be) completely insensitive to behaviors that are likely to escalate into harmful actions.

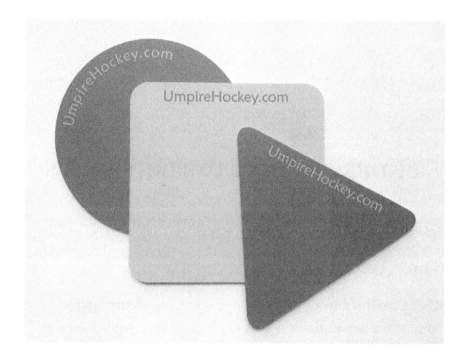

4

UNDERSTANDING UMPIRE SIGNALS

SIGNALS

Three Types of Signals

There are three types of signals: primary, secondary, and administrative. Primary signals come first; they show everyone what happens next and are most important to maintaining the game's flow. With the advent of the self-start option, it is more critical than ever to "show-and-hold" primary signals immediately after whistling.

THE MOST IMPORTANT primary signal is DIRECTION. It answers the athlete's question, *"Which way do I go?!?"*

Secondary signals are of secondary importance and show

everyone what happened in the past. If a secondary signal is used, it is to be shown AFTER the primary signal.

Showing a secondary signal before a primary signal stalls the game and breaks down flow. Coaches and fans should watch for this as a way to assess the level of training an umpire brings to the game.

An umpire who shows secondary signals prior to primary signals should only be umpiring sub-varsity games.

Administrative signals are those used to communicate that time should start and stop, how much time is left to play, and when players are violating distance requirements.

In 2002, I coined the labels "primary signals" and "secondary signals" for use in the clinics I hold with experienced umpires as a means to help them break the bad habit of showing secondary signals first. Happily, use of these labels has spread rapidly and is now rather commonplace around the globe. I'm proud of that! Not just because I coined the terms but because they have proven to be an effective training tool and as a result more umpires are showing primary signals first, which improves the flow of the game and therefore advances hockey.

 UMPIRES: *Showing secondary signals first is an easy habit to break—just don't show any secondary signals for at least three games.*

Coaches sometimes want to know what happened ("What was that for?" they shout out) but, umpires are not there to help the coaches understand what the umpires saw. Coaches are there to observe their players and see if the players are performing the actions they were coached to do.

Umpires are there to facilitate play. Umpires are there for the athletes and the athletes typically only want to know one thing, *"Which way do I go?!?"* Umpires answer that most important question and facilitate an open and flowing game by giving primary signals first.

I've heard coaches ask, *"How can I teach my players to get better if you don't show me what they're doing wrong?"* For umpires, that question is typically a euphemism for, *"How can I disagree with your call if you don't show me what you're calling?"*

Umpires officiate games to facilitate play, not to teach coaches by giving a history lesson for every call.

Further, umpires tend to be on the run and don't always have time to give a secondary signal. Besides, there isn't a secondary signal for every violation. For example, there is no secondary signal for an attack player entering into the circle on a Penalty Corner before the ball is inserted. Nor is there a secondary signal for a similar violation for the defense. There is also no secondary signal for the inserter not having one foot outside the field of play. That no secondary signals exist for fouls that take place during one of the most important parts of the game highlight just how secondary the secondary signals are. One could argue that they are almost completely unnecessary.

The umpires should, however, have a sense of when they should show a secondary signal—an important call (during a carding, giving or ending a Penalty Corner as time is expiring, when there appears to be legitimate confusion, etc.). And, while it is a bad 'mechanic' for umpires to always show secondary signals, umpires should be sensitive to when showing a secondary signal will help the enjoyment of the game for fans.

As noted, the most important signal is to tell the athlete's to, *"Play on!"* This verbal instruction can be enhanced by pointing down at the ground with an open hand, palm to the play. *"Play on,"* is the only loud public announcement an umpire would typically give during a game. It tells everyone that the umpire saw what people might think is a foul but decided that it isn't a foul so the umpire announces, *"Play on!"*

A high clear from a goalkeeper that pops up and goes over everyone's head often gets everyone's attention but it is seldom dangerous. When an umpire does nothing, the fans think that the umpire is blind. Umpires should let everyone know that their eyesight is fine, that they see the ball way up in the air, and, if it isn't thought to be dangerous, say, *"Play on,"* in a firm, confident voice. Umpires can even add, *"Not dangerous,"* to the announcement. Umpires can bet lots of people are asking, *"Isn't that dangerous?"*

The second most important signal is the signal that tells everyone that the umpire is holding the whistle for advantage. The umpire raises his/her arm and points down the competition surface in the direction that the team he/she is going to award possession to is attacking.

The third most important signal typically begins with a whistle. It is called direction. It tells everyone which team gets the ball and it is way more important than any secondary signal. There is no whistle if the direction signal is used when the ball goes out of bounds.

Other primary signals include the signals for penalties and set plays, i.e. a hit in from the 23-meter line, Penalty Corner, and Penalty Stroke. As is the case with all primary signals, these signals tell the athletes what comes next.

As you can no doubt tell, the least important signals are the secondary signals. These are the signals that the umpires use to 'explain' why the whistle was blown. They should only be used when doing so enhances the game. After blowing the whistle and signaling direction, an umpire might want to indicate what the foul was by showing the appropriate secondary signal for obstruction, third-party, stick obstruction, danger, advancing, etc.

These 'explanations' should ONLY be employed when the umpire has time and feels it would be particularly helpful for the athletes in what would otherwise be an unnecessarily confusing situation. It is NOT the umpire's responsibility to answer a coach who is asking, *"What was the foul?"* Umpires do not HAVE to give secondary signals.

An umpire should almost always give secondary signals when carding a player so all the players can see what it is that they shouldn't do! This also helps the other umpire, the coaches, and the fans understand exactly what happened.

That said, there is absolutely NO reason to give 'explanation' signals after every whistle and it shouldn't be done.

IMPORTANT: Umpires should never give an explanation signal before signaling and holding to show direction. I have made that point already but it is well worth restating.

The Mechanics of Signaling

Umpires are signaling for ALL the players in the game to see and/or hear.

UMPIRES: Stick out your chest, suck in your tummy, and give your signal proudly (but with some degree of empathy). Look good when you're signaling, it's the moment an umpire might be shown on television. ☺ NEVER cross your body with your directional signal. ALWAYS keep your full chest toward the play when signaling and use an open palm.

Sometimes when signaling direction to the left the players might ask the umpire where to put the ball. If it is to the umpire's right, the umpire should not point for the placement until he or she has stopped showing direction. If the umpire is giving direction to the left and at the same time pointing out placement on the right, the umpire will be pointing in two different directions and it can be confusing.

Whenever I indicate ball placement, I try to make sure I do so with a look that is much different when giving a directional signal. I will often point down at the ground with my hand below my waist, with an open hand. This is clearly no directional signal.

Signaling Style

There is a difference between signaling mechanics and an umpire's individual style. The end position of all arm signals is dictated in the *Rules of Hockey*. How an umpire gets to that defined end position, is individual style. Umpires are not allowed to change the end position but they can do almost anything on the way there.

I know a very tall umpire who signals Penalty Corners by bringing his arms into position via a huge windmill fashion, locking each arm into place in their finishing position, one after another. His end position for both arms is pointing at the goal with both arms fully extended and parallel to the ground—a perfect Penalty Corner signal done with style and flair.

On the other hand, I know an umpire who signals a Penalty Corner by reaching down and holding her hands down at the ground—it looks like she's trying to tie her shoes. That is simply NOT a Penalty Corner signal. I know another umpire who puts both his arms over his head like the officials do in American football to signal touchdown—that is NOT a Penalty Corner signal either. Those umpires are exhibiting bad mechanics.

Most of the time, umpires are just running around watching the play…

But, sometimes they have to blow their whistle and make a call! Let's take a look at primary and secondary signals, what they look like, and explain why they're used.

Primary Signals Show Everyone What Comes Next

ADVANTAGE: The advantage signal is shown to let everyone know that the umpire saw a breach but the umpire, rather than blowing the whistle, is waiting to see if the team going in the direction the umpire is pointing would be better off if play is allowed to continue. The arm, pointing in the direction of the team that is to have possession of the ball, is held up in the air, well above shoulder height.

ADVANTAGE

Notice that the umpire's hand is open, palm facing the players. Notice too that she is not reaching across her body. When her right arm is up, it will be the team attacking to the umpire's right that will get the ball if she blows the whistle. If her left arm were up, the team attacking to the umpire's left would get the ball if she were to have to blow the whistle.

DIRECTION: If the umpire blows the whistle, the teams have to know which way to go!

The direction signal is performed immediately following the whistle and before any secondary signal.

If the team attacking to the umpire's left commits a breach, and there is no advantage to award, the umpire will blow the whistle and show direction for the team attacking to the right. In this case, the umpire holds their right arm up at shoulder height, parallel to the ground, and pointing towards the goal on the umpire's right. If the breach is against the other team, then the umpire points at the other goal, i.e. in the other direction.

The reason the umpire points at the goal, and not just 'down the sideline' is to ensure their arm isn't hidden behind their body from nearby players (on the non-pointing side).

Sometimes, especially just after halftime, umpires will momentarily point in the wrong direction. When they do, they should ensure both teams are ready to go in the opposite direction so as not to give either team an unfair advantage based on an unintended pointing error.

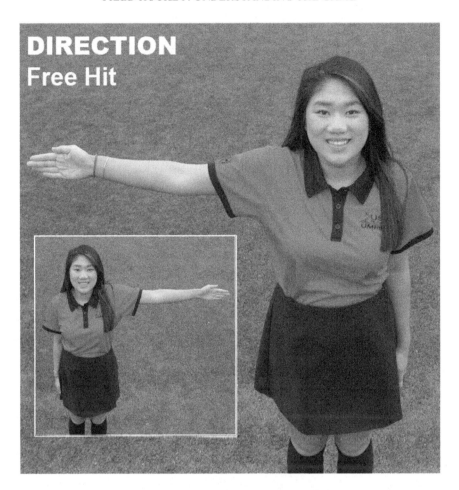

As with the advantage signal, the umpire's palm is open, facing the players, and she is not reaching across her body. A well-trained umpire strives to make it easy for all the players (and fans) to see which way to go.

Play is restarted from a point within playing distance of where the breach occurred.

DIRECTION (ball over sideline): When the ball crosses to the outside of one of the sidelines, the umpire – without blowing the whistle – holds up one arm, shoulder height, parallel to the ground, and points down at the sideline with the other arm. The arm that the umpire holds up is used to point at the goal that the team is attacking that didn't last touch the ball before it left the field of play. Given the photograph on this page, the team attacking to the umpire's right last touched the ball so she is pointing to the goal on her left.

Play is restarted where the ball crossed the sideline.

DIRECTION
Ball Over Sideline

NOTE: *The umpire should blow the whistle if the ball goes out of bounds and players are still contesting the ball for possession.*

HIT IN DEFENSE: Another boundary ball is one that goes over either of the backlines. If a ball goes across a backline after it was last touched by the team that was attacking that end of the field, the umpire doesn't blow the whistle – unless the athletes are still fighting for the ball – but does hold both arms up, parallel with the backline. The palms of both hands are open and facing the centerline. This signal is commonly known as a "16" because the athlete restarting play can do so from as many as 16 yards away from the backline.

Play is restarted where the ball crossed the backline or up to 16-yards from the backline, in line with where the ball left the field.

HIT IN DEFENSE (or 16)
Ball Over Backline

NOT SHOWN: If the defense last touches the ball before it crosses a backline, the umpire shows direction (always to his/her right) by pointing to where the ball crossed the line and 'drawing' a line between that spot and the 23-meter line. The attack puts the ball on the 23-meter line, in line with where the ball crossed the backline, and restarts play from there.

PENALTY CORNER: When the defense accidentally breaches the rules inside the circle and the breach didn't impact a scoring play, the umpire blows the whistle and signals a Penalty Corner. A Penalty Corner is also awarded if the defense intentionally breaches the rules when the ball is outside the circle and within 25 yards of the backline (in indoor hockey, an intentional breach by the defense outside the circle but inside the half of the court the defense is defending is a Penalty Corner). Another reason the umpire penalizes the defense with a Penalty Corner is when the defense intentionally plays the ball over the backline. The umpire signals a Penalty Corner by pointing both hands at the goal with arms extended and parallel to the ground. Timekeepers must stop the clock when this signal is shown.

Play is restarted from the backline, inside the circle but not less than 10 meters from the closest goal post. Attack selects side.

[NFHS (10.2.1): The clock is not stopped for Penalty Corners and, unless there is damage to the surface, the ball must be placed 10 yards from the goal post.]

PENALTY STROKE: When the defense intentionally breaches the rules inside the circle or when an accidental breach stops a goal, the umpire blows the whistle and signals a Penalty Stroke. The umpire signals a Penalty Stroke by pointing one hand at the penalty stroke mark, which is 7 yards/6.4 meters from the center of the goal-line, with the other hand held high above the head. The clock must stop when this signal is shown.

Play is restarted from the Penalty Stroke mark.

PENALTY STROKE

UMPIRES: When signaling a Penalty Corner or Penalty Stroke, more often than not, you should give a secondary signal explaining what breach occurred (if there is one for the breach in question) because these penalties greatly increase the likelihood that a goal will be scored and everyone watching the game will want to know what happened.

GOAL: When a team scores, the umpire blows the whistle and points with both hands to the center of the field; arms parallel to the ground. The signal is consistent with telling the players what comes next and which way to go. With this signal the umpire is saying, *"A goal has been scored and I'm pointing where play will restart."*

Play is restarted midway between the sidelines and backlines.

"GOOOOOOOAL"

BULLY: The final, and probably rarest primary signal is to tell the players that play will restart with a bully. A bully is called when play is forced to stop and no breach of the rules occurred.

There are two ways umpires signal a bully. One is to alternately move the hands up and down like a juggler at a carnival. The other, see photograph, is to mimic the bully action by alternately moving the hands up and down and touching them together.

Secondary Signals Show Everyone What Happened

After an umpire shows the primary signal, you might notice an additional, secondary signal.

Secondary signals show people what happened, however, their use to demonstrate obvious breaches of the rules is frowned upon. For example, if a lone player kicks the ball to a teammate and only a person who wasn't watching the play would have missed it – a secondary signal should not be shown.

The umpires should use these signals when they have time and feel there might be confusion about why the whistle was blown. Some of these signals are known by other names such as "Third-Party Obstruction" and "Stick Interference". The secondary signals are presented below…

Kicked ball

Dangerous play

Encroachment

Back of Stick

NOTE: "Encroachment" is the least self-explanatory secondary signal. It is shown when opponents are too close to free hits, when teammates are too close to free hits inside the attacking quarter, and when an attacking team enters the circle from a free hit within the attacking quarter without first meeting the requirements of indirect circle entry.

Body obstruction

Stick obstruction

Obstruction by an offball teammate

Illegally raised ball

NOTE: *The "illegally raised ball" signal is used when the ball is raised into the air using the hitting action when not a shot on goal and when the hitting action is used to take the first shot on a Penalty Corner and the ball rises on a path to cross the goal-line above 18 inches (or crossed the goal-line above 18 inches).*

Pushing (simulate pushing)

Administrative Signals

The most important administrative signal is to stop the clock. Okay, you could argue that this is a primary signal because the umpire is indicating what comes next but, because it is used to communicate with the timekeeper, let's put it into this category.

STOP CLOCK/TIMEOUT: To tell the timekeeper to stop the game clock, besides whistling to signal Penalty Corners and Penalty Strokes, umpires blow their whistle and cross their wrists above their head (though many don't quite get the X up over their head). The clock can be stopped by the umpire at their discretion, for example when there is an injury, lightning, or an animal comes onto the field. The palms of the both hands are open and facing the center of the field. There are no team timeouts in NCAA or FIH games. The clock is stopped when video is used to review an important play.

[NFHS (4.1.3): Only in NFHS games can a team call a timeout to pause the competition. Each team is permitted one 90-second timeout per game.]

VIDEO REVIEW: An administrative signal was created for use for a video review of a call (or lack of a call).

The umpire begins by signaling timeout. Then, if the team is asking for the referral, they use their arms to make a big T in front of their torso (the T stands for Team) and then, using two hands, they draw a large rectangle in the air (like a video display screen). Umpires can ask for a video review too. In such a case, the big T is replaced by pointing to themselves as if to say, "This is my timeout."

Most other administrative signals are seldom used. For example, in the olden days, before giant scoreboards that display the official time, umpires used to hold up two hands with one finger on each hand pointed towards the sky to indicate that there were two minutes remaining in the half. I'm certain you can guess what it meant when the umpires held up one hand with one finger pointed to the sky.

CHAPTER 5

UNDERSTANDING THE RULES

One of the hardest and easiest things about officiating hockey games in the USA is that hardly anyone involved in the sport has a very good understanding of the rules. This extends to include coaches, players, parents, fans, and, sadly, some umpires. Complicating things for casual observers is that not every violation of the rules should be penalized.

Most people in the USA are used to the idea that an umpire is simply a police officer charged with enforcing the rules or a surgeon charged with operating on a patient to eliminate every single cancer cell. In hockey, however, the umpire is asked to be a judge first and, only if necessary, to be a police officer or surgeon.

The hockey umpire sees, on a good day, almost every infraction and judges whether any given infraction should be penalized—did the breach have an impact or is it best to let it go?

Officiating hockey is not a simple black-and-white reading of the rules. While there are some absolutes (for example, did the whole ball cross the side-line), hockey umpires make decisions based on whether anyone was disadvantaged by the breach and current practices, interpretations, and special instructions and guidance given at a pre-season/pre-tournament briefing. If an umpire blows his or her whistle for every single breach of the rules, they'll absolutely ruin the game in the process.

An umpire sits in judgment (for a hundredth of a second), decides privately, and 'demonstrates' his or her decision by whistling or, just as important, by NOT taking action.

Coaches and spectators, and sometimes players, often misunderstand when a rule is broken and the umpire has decided to not take any action. This is when umpires hear rude comments like, *"Are you blind?"* or *"You're missing a good game."* If a player or coach were to make a comment like that, the umpire must warn that person with a card.

The umpire is under no obligation to announce that he or she has decided not to penalize a breach but experienced umpires will learn when it is a good time to do so.

Many times it is more advantageous to the team being fouled to allow the athletes to play on, working through fouls to the resolution of the play—a better opportunity for a shot on goal might be just another step away. This is why you'll hear coaches tell their players to, *"Play to the whistle."* Of course, the athlete shouldn't have to fight through every foul just to see if they might get something better in the end. That can be too frustrating. An umpire, a good one, is like an artist—facilitating play by knowing when and when not to blow the whistle.

The resulting 'advantage' of a situation typically becomes clear only after one team has gained possession or a significantly advantageous position in the game. In the meantime, the ball may have traveled 5 to 10 meters away from the place of the foul. This can be very confusing for the fans.

FANS: A sprinting player collects a ball as it rolls into an open space and, without breaking stride, the player begins what will be a beautiful breakaway. Suddenly, the umpire blows his or her whistle to stop the play and gives possession to the other team. The fans ask in disbelief, *"What was that?"*

What happened was quite simple. Noah and Aaron were battling for possession of the ball. Noah stepped in for better footing and accidentally booted the ball to a wide open space 10 meters away. The umpire saw this but didn't blow the whistle because the umpire was awaiting the outcome of the play. Noah's teammate sprinted forward and began dribbling on a breakaway. Not fair! Noah kicked the ball to the disadvantage of Aaron's team. The umpire makes things fair again by blowing the whistle and taking the ball away from the team that kicked it. The umpire penalized Noah's team by giving Aaron's team possession.

This example clearly illustrates one of the ways that the game of hockey can be very frustrating for those who have only an elementary understanding of the rules.

QUESTION: **What if one of Aaron's teammates had received the ball instead?**

ANSWER: **The umpire should not blow the whistle.**

Preparation

Being able to give the combatants the best when officiating their game is a combination of mental and physical preparation.

PHYSICAL FITNESS

High school athletes are working to improve their game in winter indoor programs, spring clubs, summer camps, pre-season practices, and every day during the season. Umpires should be training too. How fast can the athletes run the 40-yard dash? How many dashes will the athletes run during a game? If you're going to umpire, you have to be physically fit to be fair!

NOTE: Always check with a physician before beginning a fitness program.

How does an umpire measure their physical readiness? USA Field Hockey feels that an umpire officiating high school games should be able to run two miles in no more than 17 minutes. There are several fitness tests umpires can consider:

1. The Hockey Ladder (speed and agility – measure time to complete a specially designed shuttle run using distances on a hockey pitch, detailed description and video on UmpireHockey.com/fitness)

2. The Hockey Pitch Run (endurance – run around a hockey pitch for 8 minutes and record number of laps, to the nearest quarter lap)

3. The Coopers 12-Minute Run (endurance – measure distance covered in 12 minutes on a 400 meter track)

4. The Beep Test (endurance – measure completed trips)

While we're on the subject of umpire fitness, I feel it worth reminding everyone of the comparison chart showing what high school athletes did while competing in hockey back in 1987 with what a typical 2014 college-bound athlete does to prepare. In the old days, high school athletes didn't play very much hockey during the year. That has all changed. Now, hockey athletes are training and competing year round (they're faster with and without the ball). In addition, more and more games are being played on synthetic surfaces (the game is faster) and with the introduction of the self-start, the game hardly ever stops.

 UMPIRES: Whether you've just started learning how to umpire hockey or can count your officiating experience in decades, your speed, agility and endurance—your level of fitness—matters more than the level of fitness found in umpires of yesteryear.

SUBJECT MATTER EXPERTISE

Surprising that I even have to say this but, umpires are supposed to know the rules—even the little ones. If an umpire is wrong about one rule, people will naturally question that umpire's knowledge about ALL the rules.

Interpretations

More important than knowing the rules is *understanding* the rules. Keep current! This isn't just for umpires. Players and coaches have to understand the current rule interpretations so they have an appropriate expectation of what an umpire is thinking/considering and likely to do during a game.

UMPIRES: Making the current interpretations part of your game isn't just important—it's critical!

Umpires do get to establish their own officiating style/flair. Umpires do NOT get to invent personal interpretations that are different from the person whose title is, typically, Interpreter. If you want to umpire and you played hockey twenty years ago and you think players shouldn't be allowed to turn around and spin when they're dribbling or ever raise the stick above their shoulders as they prepare to hit the ball, too bad! An umpire doesn't get to call the game 'their' way because that was 'the' way they remember it was being called when they played.

SCOUTING

One of the best ways umpires can prepare for a big game is hardly ever used—scout the teams! The more important an upcoming game is, the more important it is to scout. How does the team attack? Do they leave an attacker up field with the opponent's goalkeeper? What type of Penalty Corners do they run? Are they a physical team? Do their defenders tackle from behind? Does their coach misbehave? Do they do a lot of aerials? How do they defend aerials? Do they swing wildly? Were the umpires that were calling the game effective? If so, what worked? If not, what might be done differently? If an umpire can't scout the teams, they should learn as much as they can about the teams and the game—learn whether the teams are rivals and what happened the last time the teams played each other, if it is an important game learn what's at stake.

Knowledge gained from scouting won't change how an umpire will officiate but it can help the umpire develop an action plan that is mindful of the game's particular set of circumstances.

PSYCHOLOGICAL

Umpires have to concentrate for the entire game. There are times when the most amazing plays happen in the first few minutes when the players have the most energy. Unprepared umpires might be heard to say, *"I was just getting warmed up."*

There are times when umpires can relax a bit but, for the most part, they have to really be concentrating.

 UMPIRES: Are you ready? Are you having a bad day? Trouble at home/school? Can you clear your mind?

Some umpires will visualize special circumstances before starting a game. Better to be surprised in a visualization then by something that actually happens in a game!

Basic Umpiring Skills

WHISTLING

Do you know how to blow a whistle? I mean, with skill, purpose, and in a way that communicates with 22 hockey athletes? It's not as easy as one might think and most new umpires have to be taught.

STEP 1: Block the whistle's opening with your tongue, blow hard but do not remove your tongue. Do exactly that a couple of times.

STEP 2: Block the whistle's opening with your tongue, blow hard and a moment later, retract your tongue from the opening and stop blowing after appropriate 'amount' of noise has left whistle.

The start of the noise should be like an explosion. It is instantaneous. Whistling in sport does NOT involve a slow release of the air in your lungs.

The end of the sound should not trail off like a train whistle fading away in the distance. The ending should be abrupt, sharp.

Remember, the umpire is typically blowing the whistle to alert ALL the players in the game about something. The whistle is used by the umpire to insert him or herself into the action in a very definitive manner. Don't whimper. WHISTLE!

Umpires use their whistle to communicate. They have to learn how to 'talk' to the players with their whistle. Here are different 'conversations' umpires might want to have using their whistle.

"Psst. I need to tell you something." The whistle is blown a couple/few times; not as powerfully as one might for a foul. It should sound a bit like three small fire crackers going off in quick succession. The umpire would do this when indicating that a ball has gone out of bounds and there are athletes nearby who think that the ball is still in play.

"Hey! Don't do that again!" The whistle should be LOUD and LONG when a foul is particularly unpleasant, for example a sloppy play with physical contact, stopping a breakaway with a bad tackle from behind, etc. In other words, next time the umpire sees that (maybe even THIS time) there will be a card for that behavior. This is the type of infraction that the umpire is telling everyone (all the players, the coaches, and even the fans) that they've seen something that better not happen again!

IMPORTANT: When a defender fouls an attacker within the attacking 23 meter area and the support umpire uses a long, loud whistle to make the call; this is a signal to the managing umpire that awarding a Penalty Corner is appropriate. The responsible umpire should turn and signal Penalty Corner as soon as he or she hears the support umpire's long, loud whistle (the support umpire does NOT signal the Penalty Corner). If either team doesn't seem to know that a Penalty Corner has been awarded, then the lead should pop his or her whistle a couple/few times to say, "Look at me," and then reinforce the Penalty Corner signal.

HOLDING THE WHISTLE

There are two meanings to the phrase "holding the whistle" in hockey officiating. The first refers to the mechanics of how the umpire holds the whistle in his or her hand. The second refers to what we also call "holding for advantage" and it is a major part of the hockey umpire's responsibility—this is also what can cause confusion for fans. They see a foul but the foul isn't called (they might hear the umpire yell out, *"Play on!"*) or they don't see a foul and the umpire seemingly blows the whistle for no reason at all.

An umpire does NOT blow his or her whistle every single time there is a violation of the rules—sometimes, the umpire 'puts the whistle on hold' instead of blowing it. They 'hold' to see if it would help the team that was fouled to let play continue rather than interrupting the game with a whistle.

Physically – Umpires hold the whistle so it will be ready to use (and won't be dropped) or they wear whistles that attach to their fingers.

The whistle should be held. It should not be hung around the neck on a lanyard and never carried in the mouth (good for basketball, bad for hockey).

Umpires should not hold the whistle up near their mouth. If they do, they'll look indecisive (are they going to blow it or not) and childish—like a baby sucking on a pacifier or their thumb.

Worse, umpires who carry the whistle in their mouth, or near their mouth, are likely to blow the whistle too quickly.

I recommend that umpires connect a 'tooter' whistle or pen to their main whistle.

This way the umpires will have two different sounding whistles in case they're asked to officiate a tournament with games going on side-by-side. Further, the other whistle serves as a handle and, I think, makes the whistles easy to find in an umpiring bag.

I'm a little uncomfortable using a whistle with finger grip but...

...they're perfectly fine and have at least one big advantage, especially for beginners. The fact is that they can't be held in a way that covers the air holes nor can they be put into the mouth with the air holes facing the ground. Both of those mistakes dampen and/or distort the sound.

With whistle(s) in their hand, the umpires can signal advantage (point down field) and then, after deciding they must blow the whistle, they move their hand to their mouth and blow the whistle—simple.

I find no credible reason that the whistle is best held in the right or left hand (there are some who believe the left hand is a near requirement). On average, 50% of the calls will be for the team going to the left and the other 50% will be calls for the team going to the right. I would say that carrying the whistle with the non-dominant hand might help slow an umpire's whistling down a bit but, not significantly. Umpires should hold the whistle in whichever hand they are most comfortable.

The whistle should be held from the back. If the whistle is held on the sides, holes can be accidentally covered which radically changes or virtually eliminates the noise that the whistle is supposed to generate.

The holes should be up, away from the body, helping the noise travel away from the body and into the field of play.

Mentally – Holding the whistle for advantage (putting the whistle 'on hold' and waiting for the play to develop).

The more an umpire officiates the more they'll learn NOT to blow the whistle. They'll learn that it is almost always beneficial to the team that was fouled to hold (not blow) the whistle.

Less skilled umpires will blow their whistle too much. Beginning umpires will typically never blow their whistle at first—and then start blowing too much. The good news is that beginners start by officiating games where a quick whistle won't be a critically bad thing—and in lower level games the players might actually benefit from a few more interruptions. Regardless, umpires must have the confidence NOT to blow their whistle for at least a full second to see if things work out to the advantage of the team that was fouled. In short, even new umpires officiating at the lowest levels of the game should begin holding for advantage.

 UMPIRES: Whenever you're holding for advantage, hold your arm up pointing in the direction that the team that will get the ball is attacking. If you hold for advantage, you cannot award possession in the opposite direction for a foul that happens while you're holding for advantage.

NIGHTMARES: Bad things can happen when umpires don't hold their whistle for advantage. Here are two such scenarios.

1. A defender tackles an attacker from behind. The attacker is about 30 meters out from the goal-line the defender's team is protecting. It's the world's worst stick-to-stick tackle ever. The umpire blows his/her whistle. And, to show displeasure with the defender, the umpire blows LOUD and LONG. Then, before the sound of the whistle dissipates from the arena, the ball springs forward about 20 yards to an attacker waiting at the top of the circle. Instead of having the ball in the circle, the umpire has given the attack possession back at the 35. The 'quick' whistle ends up rewarding the defense and penalizes the attack. What's worse, because the ball traveled so far from the breach, while the attack takes the ball back to the place of the foul, the Free Hit is going to take place after the entire defense has had time to set itself into proper position—a much better position than when they were chasing the breakaway

attacker! With the self-start, there are more and more reasons to blow a foul early but wouldn't it have been better in this case to see if the attacker could have worked through the foul? Some umpires are too quick to penalize. What harm would come from waiting? (The player who committed the foul just described is also to be carded on their team's next dead ball possession.)

2. An attacker breaks past a defender into the circle and dribbles towards the goalkeeper. The attacker shoots. The goalkeeper mistimed the kick to clear the ball. The ball squirts under the goalkeeper's foot and stops just behind the goalkeeper. The attacker has continued on course for the ball. As the goalkeeper starts to turn so that he or she can kick the ball out from in front of the goal, the goalkeeper is clearly obstructing the attacker—an intentional action that also keeps the attacker from getting to the ball—so the umpire blows the whistle to call his/her first Penalty Stroke. Problem is, as the goalkeeper turned, his or her heel kicks the ball and just after the umpire blew their whistle, the ball rolls into the goal. (No goal! The umpire's whistle kills the play. It's still a Penalty Stroke.)

UMPIRES: There are times when a quick whistle is very important—typically when something dangerous has or might happen.

Positioning/Line of Sight Skills

Critical to a successful outing officiating a hockey game is the positioning that the umpires use throughout the competition. Knowing when (and when not) to be in close proximity to the play is an important part of proper positioning.

This section of the book contains over a dozen graphics providing a static view of the positioning that umpires should take up during various parts of the game. The letter 'U' is used to represent each umpire. None of the diagrams are meant to suggest that the umpire is in any of the illustrated positions for a long period of time. Umpires, coaches, players, and fans can learn a little about how to assess an umpire's game based on the positioning they take during play.

Photograph by Hu Guo Wei

MOST IMPORTANT: *"Is the ball to my left?"* Umpires should repeat that question over and over again when they're officiating. The answer should almost always be yes! The few exceptions are when managing a Penalty Corner and Penalty Strokes, and when the ball is near the back-line on the far side of their goal. Oh! And when the umpire gets beaten by a surprise breakaway (which shouldn't happen very often at all).

FANS AND COACHES: Rather than judging an umpire poorly because they missed the tiny hockey ball hitting a foot in a crowded circle (that will happen), watch the umpires and ask, "Is the ball to their left?" If they often allow the ball to get on their right, you've got an umpire who needs coaching, a higher level of fitness, or better concentration.

The following graphic shows the suggested position of umpires in the attacking third of the competition surface.

The lead or managing umpire is shown within a shaded area that illustrates the places that the managing umpire will most often find himself or herself during scoring attempts. Depending upon his or her fitness and speed, and pre-game agreement with the other umpire, the support umpire might come down as far as the 23-meter line and should not hesitate to make calls in the shaded area in front of that position IF the play is leaving the circle and heading towards him/her OR the play is right next to the side-line. The umpires will discuss these situations prior to the game.

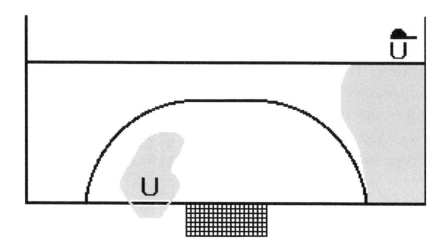

TEAM WORK: The trail or support umpire in the hat (above) should blow the whistle LONG and LOUD when a player defending a left side attack intentionally fouls inside the attacking 23 meter area of the competition surface but outside the circle. This long and loud whistle signals the managing umpire that the support umpire (in the hat) feels that a Penalty Corner should be awarded.

FIRST, LET'S ELIMINATE THE NEGATIVE

Bad Positioning

The next two graphics are designed to illustrate why the umpires should NOT position themselves "even with"(or in front of) a Free Hit.

THE HIT: The Black Dots, the team in black, are preparing to take a Free Hit (see arrow for attacking direction) and, as you can see, the umpire has positioned himself or herself to be "even with" the position of the play. Taking up that position is not a good idea. Some umpires are even seen positioning themselves to the side and in front of the ball (further away

from the back-line) than the umpire in the illustration. This puts
the ball on the umpire's right. That's bad. The ball should be on
the umpire's left.

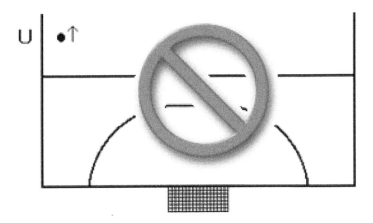

THE STEAL: Just as the Black Dots restart play, a player from
the White Dots intercepts and immediately passes to a
teammate cutting to the top of the circle.

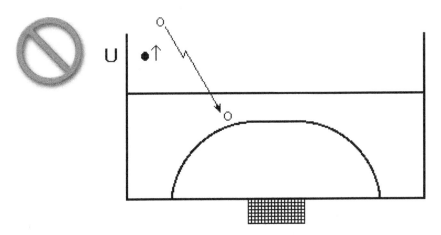

This puts the ball 20 to 25 meters to the umpire's right and
leaves the umpire in no position to judge whether a slow rolling
shot on goal that gets behind the goalkeeper goes completely

over the goal-line. Had the umpire been 'behind' the Free Hit with the play to his or her left and "protecting" the area to his or her right, the umpire would be in better position for the interception and resulting scoring opportunity.

FANS: Have you seen umpires getting trapped by taking a position too high on the Free Hit? The umpires should position themselves so as to be in position to cover the area to their right by keeping the ball on their left!

SECOND, LET'S EMPHASIZE THE POSITIVE

Good Positioning

The next two graphics are designed to illustrate proper positioning during Free Hits near the 23-meter line. The position of the players will influence the exact position the umpire takes prior to the play.

In the first of the two graphics, the umpire has taken a position behind the play, but not too far from the side-line, so he or she has the ball to his or her left. The umpire will be ahead of a reversal of possession and also be ready to judge whether a ball hit far up the competition surface crosses completely over his or her side-line.

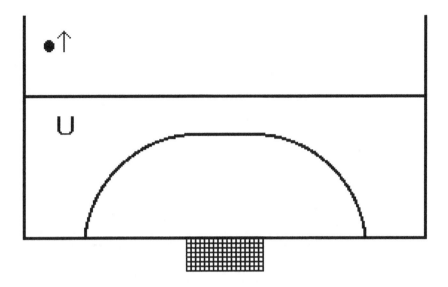

Next is a Free Hit for the White Dots. Note that the managing umpire, without the hat, has positioned himself or herself far in front of the hit and that the support umpire has come into view as he or she has moved to improve his or her proximity to the upcoming play.

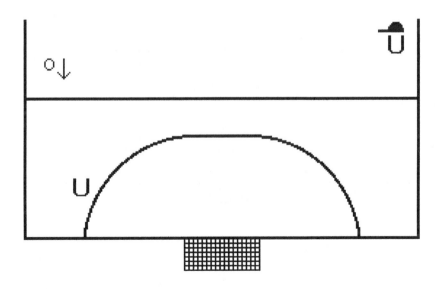

The following set of graphics is designed to illustrate the officiating team's positioning during an open field attack approaching the circle from the right and left sides.

Please note the slight variation to the umpires' positions, particularly the managing umpire (the one without the hat).

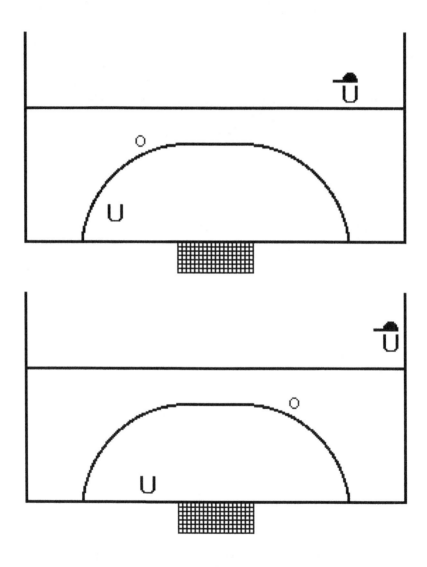

The next two graphics illustrate positioning during near and far-side Penalty Corner insertions. The support umpire (positioning NOT to scale, he or she would be at about the 45 yard line), wearing hat, watches for "suicide" runs by the defenders, high hits by the attack, and helps the managing umpire judge whether a shot has been deflected.

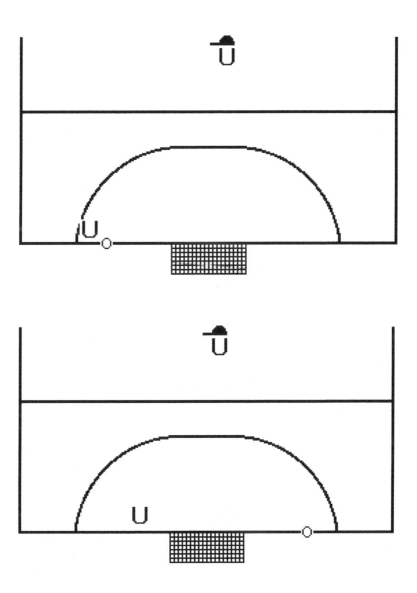

The following two graphics were designed to illustrate positioning during side-ins from both sidelines. When the ball moves away from the umpire, the umpire moves to follow the ball. It is almost as if the ball and umpire work like magnets— sometimes attracting each other (when ball moves away from the umpire, the umpire follows) and sometimes repelling each other (as the ball moves toward the umpire, the umpire is 'pushed' away).

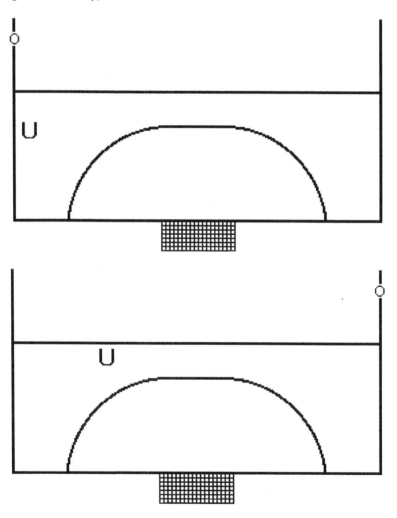

The next two graphics illustrate the officiating team's positioning during plays starting near the corners of the pitch. As in the illustration about Penalty Corners, the support umpire shouldn't be THIS close to the 23-meter line. A position about 35 yards from the back-line would be more appropriate.

In the first example, the first bit of action will take place JUST outside the circle. The lead stands facing the circle, with his or her left shoulder 'pointing' at the ball. If the ball is hit hard, the action will be in the circle so, the umpire wants his or her body prepared for play in the circle. If the attack starts with a self-start, the umpire simply 'opens up' to the play. The managing umpire must instantly move into the circle as soon as the ball does. The support umpire, wearing hat, does NOT watch the hit. He or she is watching for misconduct near or by the goalkeeper.

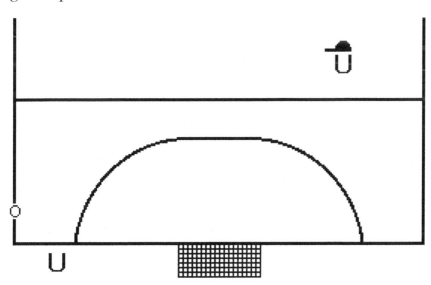

The support umpire in the graphic below, wearing hat, moves away from side-line for better view of action that will take place in front of his or her position as the ball crosses into the circle.

He or she is ready to make calls directly in front of his or her position and assist the managing umpire if the lead asks for assistance. This might happen as play enters the side of the circle closest to the support umpire's position.

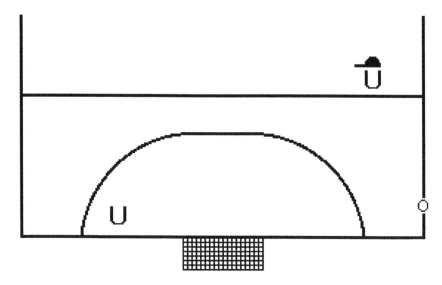

The four graphics that follow are designed to illustrate positioning when play is moving away from the circle from different points on the competition surface.

The umpire needs to be ready for interceptions with play returning to the circle while at the same time be ready to get to the side-line. However, the umpire should NOT start outside of the competition surface!

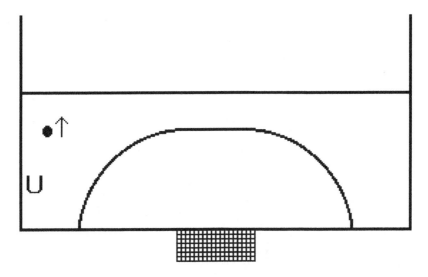

As the ball moves across the competition surface, the umpire does too. The ball remains on the umpire's left...

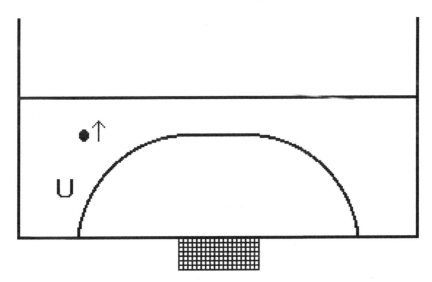

...and as the ball nears a position in front of the first post of the goal, the umpire is likely to find himself or herself inside the circle.

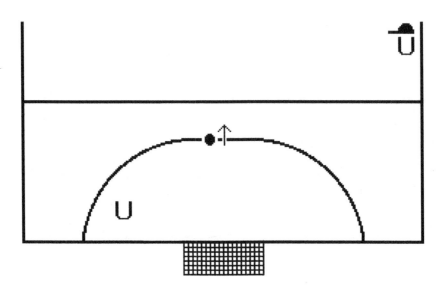

Compare the position of the ball and the umpire near the right side-line in this last graphic in the series with the graphic showing the ball on the left. This graphic helps to highlight how both umpires change their positions as the ball moves to different locations.

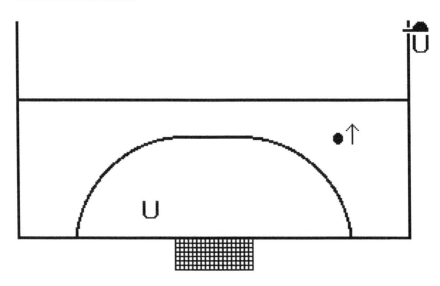

A FUNDAMENTAL TRUTH: The Ball and The Lines

With one exception, the ball is considered 'in' or 'out' only when the entirety of the ball has passed beyond the vertical plane that extends from the line into space.

The exception is that the ball is considered 'in the circle' when any part of the ball is within the plane of the circle-line (even when the ball is sent over the circle with an aerial). To be considered "out of the circle" the entire downward extension of the ball has to cross over the entire upward plane of the circle-line, back-line or goal-line. Umpire positioning is critical. Obviously, if the umpire is looking at a ball that is crossing the circle line from far enough away, it will appear to cross the line before it actually has.

Assuming that the ball has been touched inside the circle, is this a photograph of a goal?

Detail from photograph by Wolfgang Sternberger

Is the umpire in good position to judge whether the ball has crossed the line?

Photograph by Wolfgang Sternberger

Starting / Restarting Play (Dead-ball Situations)

Some umpires will 'over engineer' relatively minor restarts of play (like making sure the ball sits completely motionless when a Free Hit is taken with absolutely no one around) and not do a good enough job of managing major ones (like allowing attackers to sneak into the circle before the ball is put into play on Penalty Corners or allowing a drag flick on a Penalty Stroke). The following descriptions should help everyone understand what's important (and what's not) in specific parts of the game.

CENTER-PASS

At the beginning of each period and after each goal, the ball is put into play from the center of the competition surface. The center pass may be hit, pushed, or lifted (including any of those actions as part of a self-start) in any direction after the umpire blows his or her whistle.

Only the player who will start play can be on either side of the center-line. All the other players must be on their own side of the center-line.

Until the ball is moved, players from the team without possession must be at least 5 meters away from the player starting or restarting the game with the center-pass.

An opponent will often stand right next to the player starting the center-pass. This player is typically standing in a 'dormant' manner and is clearly not intending to interfere with the play. Obviously, the umpires can have this player move the appropriate distance away before blowing the whistle to start play but, they might also just leave the player there and watch for any subsequent benefit from the positioning.

FOULS TO WATCH FOR: Athletes who run across the center-line after the whistle and before the ball is put into play. Encroachment by defenders that disadvantages the attacking team.

SIDE-IN

When a ball goes out of bounds over a side-line, the team that did not touch the ball last restarts play with a Side-In. The ball should be put on the side-line very close (within playing distance) to the point where the ball crossed over the side-line.

 UMPIRES: Know the rules! I must emphasize that you do NOT call the ball out of bounds if the WHOLE ball didn't go COMPLETELY over the line! Too many

umpires call the ball out before it actually crosses the line and MANY players think that if the ball touches the line it is out. Be ready to say, "Play on. The ball is not out of bounds."

In terms of placement, it is important that the team not place the ball on the side-line in a position that is more advantageous than the exact location of where the ball crossed the line. The ball should be placed on the side-line within playing distance of where it went out of bounds.

All opponents must be 5 meters away and, if the attacking team is restarting within the attacking 23 meter area both opponents and teammates must start 5 meters away from the restarter.

If a defender is standing within 5 meters, the umpire does NOT blow the whistle and make the defense move. That stalls the attack and they're likely to lose whatever advantage they might have. Umpires should card a defending player for not getting the appropriate distance away if the defender's position stalls the attack. If a defender knocks the ball away to delay the resumption of play, card the player at the next appropriate opportunity (if the delay has allowed the defense to get into position, the defender can be carded before the attack takes their Free Hit as the attack's advantage is gone).

Predict where the ball will go. The destination of the ball and what will happen THERE, is MUCH more important than where it begins. However, because of the self-pass option, umpires cannot ignore the restarter.

FOULS TO WATCH FOR: Encroachment by defenders that influences the attack. Pushing and shoving at points of coverage. Obstructions as ball passes through points of coverage.

[NFHS: The 'away distance' is 5 yards, not 5 meters. Please note that 5 yards does not equal 5 meters. 5 yards is only 4.57 meters.]

FREE HIT (Free Push in Indoor Hockey)

When there is a foul in the game and no additional penalty is assessed, possession changes with a Free Hit or, during indoor hockey, a Free Push. The ball has to be put within playing distance of the point where the foul occurred and never in a more advantageous position than where the foul occurred with two exceptions.

1. OUTDOORS: If the attack fouls within 15 meters of the back-line within the attacking 23 meter area, the defense can restart play up to 15 meters away from the back-line, in line with where the foul occurred. If this foul took place inside the circle, the free hit can be taken anywhere inside the circle. Opponents of the restarter must be 5 meters away but if "caught" within 5 meters by a quick restart, the umpires allow play to continue as long as the opponents do not influence play before the ball travels 5 meters.

2. INDOORS: If the attack fouls within 9 meters of the back-line within the attacking half of the pitch, the defense can restart play up to 9 meters away from the back-line, in line with where the foul occurred. As with outdoors, if the attack's foul took place within the circle, the defense can restart play from anywhere inside the circle. Opponents of the restarter must be 3 meters away and if "caught" within 3 meters by a quick restart, the umpires allow play to continue as long as the opponents do not influence play before the ball travels 3 meters.

NOTE: A goalkeeper can take the free hit, inside or outside of the circle, but, use of the stick is required.

Before the ball is put back in play, it should be momentarily stationary (think, blink of an eye). Umpires shouldn't be out there with an electron microscope to ensure that all the molecules in the ball are at rest. If the ball is moving an inconsequential amount, play should continue. It's not about whether the ball has been stopped, it's about whether the restart is fair.

BIG PICTURE MOMENT: The team being penalized isn't the one taking the Free Hit. In fact, as long as the ball's movement is not changing the relative location of the restart or improving the team's next play, and it is clear that the Free Hit is starting, umpires should allow for a non-stationary preamble to the Free Hit or Free Push.

In the mid-field, as long as the team restarting play is not gaining an advantage, players, coaches, fans, and umpires shouldn't worry if the ball is put back into play a couple of meters off the position of the foul. However, umpires are directed to get more precise when Free Hits are awarded to the attack within the attacking 23 meter area.

 UMPIRES: Never concern yourself if a player places the ball on the side-line as he or she prepares to take a Free Hit for a foul that took place near the side-line, typically after which the ball rolled out of bounds. After all, the side-line is part of the competition surface. It is very FRUSTRATING for players (and umpire coaches) when umpires stall the flow of the game by stopping a player from taking a Free Hit from the side-line by making the player move the ball a few feet off the line. BAD UMPIRE!

As with a Side-In, when placing the Free Hit or Free Push, it is most important that the team not place the ball in a position that is more advantageous than the location of the foul. In all cases, the restart is to take place within playing distance (about one meter) of the foul.

All opponents must be 5 meters away from the place of the restart and when the Free Hit is the result of a foul by the defense inside the attacking 23 meter area, all players from both teams must be 5 meters away from the attacker restarting play (3 meters in indoor hockey when the defender's foul took place in the attacking side of the competition surface).

If a defender is standing within 5 meters, the umpire does NOT blow the whistle and make the defense move. That stalls the attack and they're likely to lose whatever advantage they might have. Umpire should card a defending player for not getting the appropriate distance away if the defender's position stalls the attack. If a defender knocks the ball away to delay the resumption of play, card the player at the next appropriate opportunity (if the delay has allowed the defense to get into position, the defender can be carded before the attack takes their Free Hit as the attack's advantage is gone).

Predict where the ball will go. The destination of the ball and what will happen THERE, is MUCH more important than where it begins. However, because of the self-pass option, umpires cannot ignore the restarter.

FOULS TO WATCH FOR: Encroachment by defenders. Pushing and shoving at points of coverage. Obstructions as ball passes through points of coverage.

FREE HIT/PUSH CLOSE TO THE CIRCLE

When the attack earns a Free Hit within 5 meters of the circle (or a Free Push within 3 meters of the circle during indoor hockey games), placement of the ball becomes very important and must be <u>more</u> precise than on other Free Hits or Pushes.

With the exception of the athlete restarting play, all players on both teams should be 5 meters away from the ball when the attack is restarting inside the attacking 23-meter area – unless the Free Hit is started so fast that the other player couldn't possibly get 5 meters away. When the team taking the Free Hit is the one defending the nearby circle, their teammates can be as close to the restarter as they want.

QUESTION: **The defense accidentally fouls within 5 of the circle they are defending, the attack restarts play. In the scenario described, do the other attackers have to be 5 away?**

ANSWER: **In this situation, all players from BOTH teams have to be at least 5 away but the umpire doesn't stop the taking of the restart if other players are "caught" within 5 and the attacker restarts quickly. Those players are barred from influencing the restarter.**

UMPIRES: Predict where the ball will go. The destination of the ball and what will happen when it gets THERE is MUCH more important than where it begins. However, because of the requirements that must be met before the ball enters the circle, you cannot ignore the restarter.

If the Free Hit is coming into the circle from the far side of the managing umpire's circle, the support umpire MUST watch for play on the ball from a hard hit. The ball might be deflected by a pair of opponents racing across the circle. Which player deflected it? The attacker or the defender? It is very likely that ONLY the support umpire will see that aspect of the play. However, the support umpire does NOT make the call and does not give any indication of what they saw UNLESS AND UNTIL the managing umpire asks the support umpire for assistance.

FOULS TO WATCH FOR: Encroachment by defenders or the attackers. Pushing and shoving at points of coverage. Obstructions as ball passes through points of coverage. A hit that rises into a crowded circle. Fouls just outside the circle (like a deflection off an attacker's or defender's stick that causes the ball to rise up dangerously as it goes into the circle) or a defender stopping/deflecting the ball with his or her foot.

NOTE: If a defender remains less than 5 meters away in order to stall or otherwise influence the attack, the situation demands a Penalty Corner because the defense is judged to have fouled intentionally within the attacking quarter.

BULLY

When there is an unscheduled disruption to the game (a dog runs away with the ball, a ball from another game comes onto 'this' game's competition surface, a flock of geese land on the competition surface, lightning is spotted), play is restarted with a Bully. Disruptions can also happen as a result of a mistake by the umpire. For example, if a Penalty Stroke is called because a player with goalkeeping privileges kicks the ball or if an umpire stopped play and called a Penalty Stroke because a field player stopped a shot using her stick above her shoulder. That *was* a

Penalty Stroke in the past but now it's, *"Play on!"*

[NFHS (8.2.PENALTIES.3): While the concept of simultaneous fouls is foreign to the *Rules of Hockey*, in games governed by the NFHS rules an umpire is allowed to judge misconduct fouls to have happened simultaneously. If there are simultaneous fouls in an NFHS game, play is restarted with a Bully. That said, even in NFHS games, good umpires will always decide which foul happened first. Calling fouls to be 'simultaneous' is considered a cop out.]

The numbers to remember in cases where a Bully is held are the metric 15, 5, 5, and 5. The Bully must be taken at least 15 meters away from back-lines, 5 meters away from sidelines, 5 meters away from the circle, and all players must be at least 5 meters away from the two players doing the Bully.

When a Bully is called 15 meters away from the back-line and 5 meters away from a side-line, the ball is placed within playing distance of where the ball was at the time of the interruption.

The players who will Bully are positioned so that they are straddling an imaginary line, drawn parallel to the back-lines, crossing under the spot where the Bully will be taken. The two involved players stand so that the goal they are attacking is on their left.

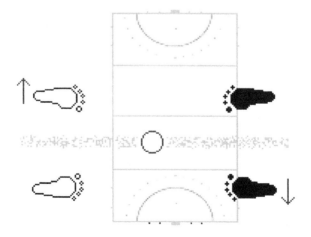

With the exception of being at least 5 meters/yards away from the spot of the Bully, the other players can be anywhere they want, scattered absolutely anywhere inside or outside the competition surface.

Penalties

The team that fouls is penalized by awarding possession to the other team. That isn't much of a penalty—it's just making things right, making things fair.

Major penalties (Penalty Corners and Penalty Strokes), however, not only provide the other team with possession but a distinct attacking advantage as a reward for having been fouled in such a way that the opponent took away an important opportunity from the attack. Said another way, penalties not only return possession to the team that was fouled, the foul is sometimes penalized by putting the fouling team at a disadvantage.

In order to penalize the defense effectively (i.c. motivate the defense not to foul), sometimes the attacking advantage is greater than it was before the foul. A Penalty Corner, for example, temporarily takes six players away from the defense and puts them back on the center-line. That's nearly a 40-yard dash (5 to 7 seconds) away from the action. Remember, moments before the foul they were defending their goal with as many as eleven players but during the Penalty Corner they can only defend their goal with a maximum of five players. That's a penalty that gives the attack a big advantage.

Details about the major penalties are provided below.

PENALTY CORNER

The following section includes very specific instructions regarding positioning and hand usage. These guidelines are important for beginning umpires to follow because they tend to

benefit from specific instructions for player management on Penalty Corners. Once an umpire is comfortable with managing Penalty Corners, and the players demonstrate by their actions that they understand what it is that the umpire wants the players to do, umpires will develop their own system/style.

Although the defense is being penalized, once a Penalty Corner is called the umpire's job is, basically, to protect the defenders as the attack prepares for the Penalty Corner insertion. Umpires CANNOT allow a Penalty Corner (or Penalty Stroke) to start before the defense is ready.

UMPIRES: After signaling a Penalty Corner, the managing umpire should:

1. *During the first couple of Penalty Corners, step into the center of the circle, on or near the Penalty Stroke mark. You should be right in front of the goal with your LEFT hand in the air signaling stop/wait. Relax this positioning with each Penalty Corner.*

2. *Make sure that the attacking team's inserter knows that he or she is NOT to restart play until you blow your whistle. However, in NFHS games, according to Rule 10, the whistle is not blown to start the Penalty Corner so make sure the inserter knows not to start until you are ready. When not using your whistle, you have to be very direct about getting the inserter's attention. If the inserter is going to the far side of the goal, call out to her/him by name or number and, when they are looking at you say, "Don't start until I let you know that I'm ready. If the inserter is going to the near side, follow them and stand in front of their insertion path and say, "When I'm ready I'll back out of your way and tell you when you can start."*

NOTE: Make sure before the Penalty Corner is put into motion that you are not standing in anyone's way. On near-side insertions, make sure you get far enough away that you won't get hit with the inserter's follow through!

Attacking teams often huddle at the top of the circle to plan their Penalty Corner attempt—more and more defending teams huddle too. It's a big moment. Planning is important.

When the defense is ready, the attack should get ready in short order BUT there is nothing in the rules governing an exact amount of time allocated for this type of discussion. Therefore, the amount of time to provide is currently the umpire's prerogative.

In all but NFHS games (see NFHS Rule 10), the clocked is stopped by the timekeeper when the umpire signals a penalty corner but, that doesn't mean that the team can take forever. Odd as it might seem, teams can still be penalized for delay of game even when the clock is stopped.

The ball MUST be put on the backline at least ten meters away from the nearest goal post, on either side of the goal at the discretion of the attacking team. The ball may not be placed outside the circle.

At least one foot of the attacker inserting the ball into play MUST be COMPLETELY beyond the back-line (at least one of the attacker's feet must be completely out of bounds) when the ball is inserted.

When everyone is ready, including the umpire, the umpire blows the whistle. At that point, the attack can begin the play and the clock is restarted by the timekeeper.

[NFHS (10.2.1): The ball MUST be put on the backline 9.14 meters (10 yards) away from the nearest goal post. Only if there is damage at or immediately in front of the insertion point can the NFHS player move the ball further from the post (never closer). Because the clock is not stopped when a Penalty Corner is signaled, NFHS umpires should be vigilant against possible delay.]

UMPIRES: The managing umpire's position is always inside the circle, closer to the near sideline than the goal. When the ball will be inserted on the 'near' side, the managing umpire is closer to the sideline than the athlete inserting the ball. Prior to the start of each Penalty Corner, the managing umpire should:

1. *Count the number of defenders. If there are not five, get a fifth (in 7v7 overtime play, only four defenders are allowed back—in such a case, make sure you have four defenders)*

2. *Ask the defenders "Are you ready?" This lets the defenders know that you're looking out for them. Before allowing the players to begin, move away and get into position (don't start the Penalty Corner while you're still backing up – first, get into position)*

3. *When everyone is ready, including yourself, blow your whistle (except, don't whistle to start Penalty Corners in NFHS games)*

4. *If time has expired (or is certain to expire during the Penalty Corner), the support umpire should come to a point that's inside the attacking 23 meter area*

Photograph by Ramon Gibert

In the two following images, the managing umpire is the one without the cap.

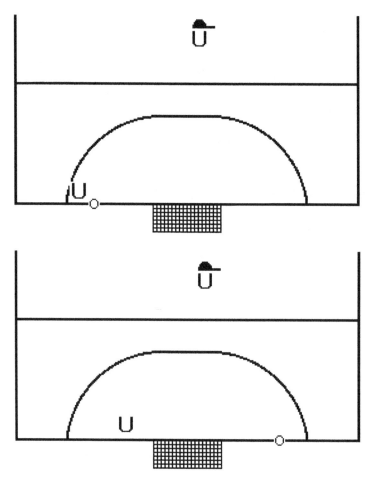

Some umpires will take a position further from the back-line. If an umpire decides to do this, they must make sure they're not in the way of any attackers. They can't assume everyone is going to run straight toward the goal. The best way for an umpire to make sure that they are not in the way to simply ask the nearest attacker, *"Am I in your way if I stand here?"* They might give the umpire a nod or ask the umpire to move a bit to the left or right. The umpire wants to position him or herself so the attackers can get by quickly. I disagree wholeheartedly with umpires who show no concern for the players, claiming that it is up to the players to get out of the umpire's way. That's rubbish.

The following image is used to highlight some common incorrect positioning taken up by the support umpire just before a Penalty Corner is started. The correct position for the support umpire to be no more than 5 meters from the center-line.

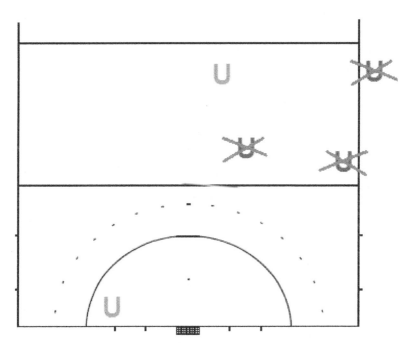

THINGS TO WATCH FOR: Dirty play (if an umpire suspects it, they can say to their partner, *"Please watch over here for misconduct fouls."*). They should say this sort of thing out loud even if they have wireless communication devices. Doing so can serve as an announcement to the players that the umpires are watching for misconduct. The attacker starting the Penalty Corner with a lift (illegal except in high school games governed by NFHS rules).

Defenders running into the circle before the attacker starts the Penalty Corner and attackers 'cheating in' before the ball is played (defenders and attackers are allowed to begin running before the ball is inserted and may break the vertical plane of the circle but may not 'touch down' in the circle until the ball has been moved). Shots from outside the circle. Defenders (including goalkeepers) using the back of the stick. Interference by attackers against defenders rushing out to defend. If the team on defense is ahead on the scoreboard, they might be interested in delaying the start of the Penalty Corner as long as possible. Repeated delays by the defense would warrant yellow cards. Will a horn sound ending the period? If so, it might prove disruptive. It's fair, though not required, for the umpire to remind the teams to, *"Play through the horn."*

NOTES: A team preparing to attack on a Penalty Corner shouldn't be rushed (for example, the attacking team's sweeper may walk up from his or her position to participate in the Penalty Corner) but the attacking team may not delay the execution of a Penalty Corner. Similarly, the defending team might make use of a speedy frontline player as their Flyer (first out). The umpire is reminded that the misconduct foul 'unnecessary delay of game' can be signaled during Penalty Corners. When delay of game is called against the attack, the umpire managing the Penalty Corner can either reverse possession (it's a big deal for the attack to lose a Penalty Corner opportunity so this better be a super clear delay of game), or the umpire can simply signal timeout and let the teams get ready—this foils any intentional attempt to delay the game. If the tactic is repeated, the umpire should signal time-out and card the delaying team's captain.

Technically, it doesn't have to be the captain who is carded but an umpire would typically 'blame' the captain for delay. To be clear, some player MUST be carded. A quick word to the captain, *"Let's move this along please. Don't delay,"* is usually all it takes to motivate the captain to get the team moving and 'signals' to everyone what's next (possible carding). A coach causing the delay (such as the coach sending in a play via a complex set of hand signals) can also cause a carding (in NFHS and NCAA games, umpires card the coach if the coach is causing a delay). One might think that if a card is given to the attacking team, that the Penalty Corner should be taken away. That is not the case. The card is separate from the already awarded Penalty Corner.

PENALTY STROKE

After signaling the Penalty Stroke and stopping their stopwatch, the umpire must make sure that the timer has actually stopped the visible clock.

Immediately after a Penalty Stroke is called, I strongly recommend new umpires meet at the top of the circle for a moment. The umpire who was in the support position should ask the umpire who called the Penalty Stroke, *"What happened?"*

This is not a challenge to the umpire who called the Penalty Stroke. This gives the umpire who called the Penalty Stroke the opportunity to articulate what the foul was. Further, it will allow the support umpire to be on the same page as the umpire who called the Penalty Stroke, because when he or she returns to his or her side of the competition surface he or she will be asked, *"Why was there a penalty stroke?"*

Both umpires will be asked the same question—they should be able to give the same answer.

Finally, and equally important, if the umpire made a mistake (for example, called a Penalty Stroke for the ball getting stuck in the goalkeeper's equipment) the partners can quickly correct the call and restart with a Penalty Corner.

QUESTION: **What penalty is awarded if the ball gets stuck in the goalkeeper's pads?**

ANSWER: **A Penalty Corner.**

The athletes who are not participating in the Penalty Stroke have to move outside of the attacking 23 meter area (relative to the goal at which the Penalty Stroke will be taken) AND make sure they move to left and right side of the competition surface so that they won't be in the defending goalkeeper's line of sight.

The umpires do NOT put the ball on the Penalty Stroke mark for the attacker. Let the attacker get the ball and place it on the stroke mark—it's the attacker's ball, not the umpires.

 UMPIRES: Regardless of the attacker's position, set yourself up with the ball on your left and within playing distance of the stroke mark, then back up a step or two away from the goal. This gives you a visual reminder of how close the attacker has to be when he or she gets ready to begin. Be sure you can see both the attacker and the goalkeeper at the same time. If you're the support umpire during the Penalty Stroke, position yourself about three meters away from the goal, on or near the back-line. Stay on the competition surface, not out of bounds—watch the attacker as they take the stroke and watch out if the shot is off target!

The umpire should give the goalkeeper and attacker time to get ready. There is no rush, time is stopped. When the umpire believes that the attacker and goalkeeper are ready (and the umpire closet to the attacker, the managing umpire, has checked with support umpire), the managing umpire blows the whistle.

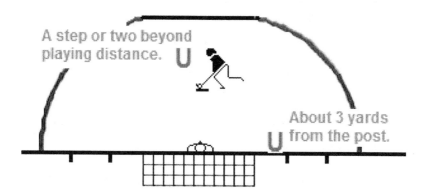

[NFHS (11.2.4): During NFHS games, the managing umpire must ask the goalkeeper and then the attacker if each is ready before blowing the whistle. A verbal response is not required but the questions must be asked aloud.]

The Penalty Stroke is a very important event. If an umpire is not sure about something (perhaps the goalkeeper takes up a strange 'ready' position), he or she should ask the players to relax and resolve the issue. At lower levels, where one tends to see lots of strange 'ready' positions, I like to ask the goalkeeper to show me his or her ready position way before the Penalty Stroke takes place so I know what it looks like when the goalkeeper is ready to defend.

It is the managing umpire's responsibility to ensure that both players are in a legal position and ready for the stroke. The support umpire's only job on a Penalty Stroke is to help the managing umpire judge whether the ball goes across the goal-line. It is not the support umpire's job to give any consideration whatsoever as to whether the goalkeeper is properly positioned on the goal-line, or if the goalkeeper leaves the goal-line prior to the shot. The managing umpire, however, might ask the support umpire to let him or her know that the goalkeeper is in proper position as part of the pre-stroke setup.

QUESTION: **Where should the goalkeeper have to be before the start of a Penalty Stroke?**

ANSWER: **The goalkeeper's feet (both feet) have to be on the goal-line (a goalkeeper who balances on the balls of his/her feet is allowed to have his/her heels above the vertical plane of the goal-line).**

If an umpire is managing a Penalty Stroke for a Under-16 or sub-varsity game, it's fair for the umpire ask the goalkeeper and attacker, *"Do you have any questions about penalty strokes before we begin? You know that after you're set neither of you can start before I blow my whistle, right?"* Properly coached players won't need an umpire's assistance but, at younger levels, it might be a necessity. Umpires might have to explain the entire situation to little kids. Time is out. It's okay. Take time. Umpires can make sure both players understand what's going to happen without coaching them. Telling a goalkeeper they have to stand on the goal-line during a Penalty Stroke is not the same as telling them they should use a slide tackle on a breakaway.

THINGS TO WATCH FOR: The attacker preparing to begin with a foot (or two) closer to the goal-line than the stroke mark. The attacker starting outside of playing distance from the ball. The attacker starting within playing distance but moving outside of playing distance after the whistle. The goalkeeper not positioning himself or herself on the goal line. The goalkeeper making his or her 'save move' before the shot. The attacker using a drag flick is NOT allowed on Penalty Strokes ('normal' flicks are). Hits are NOT allowed on Penalty Strokes but just because there's an audible tap as the ball is played does NOT mean the athlete HIT the ball. Finally, the support umpire should watch out for a shot that's wide of the goal and coming right for their head!

NOTE: Either umpire can serve as the 'managing' umpire on any given Penalty Stroke but, normally, the umpire who called the Penalty Stroke is the umpire who takes the managing position on the Penalty Stroke. The more experienced umpire can (and probably should) offer the lead position on the Penalty Stroke to the less experienced umpire especially in lower level games.

Dead-Ball Fouls

There are times when a player or coach will do something that needs to be penalized but does it when the game isn't actually in play. For example, after a whistle has been blown to indicate that a team has been awarded a Free Hit. The actions are typically small misconducts but there can be times when a player or coach earns a red card when play has stopped.

DEFENSIVE FOUL ON A FREE HIT (or Free Push)

There are two fouls that a defender, if he or she is going to foul, will typically do on a Free Hit (a Free Push during indoor hockey). One is to stay/be caught within 5 meters of the Free Hit (or 3 meters on a Free Push during indoor hockey games) and influence play without first getting more than 5 meters away. The other is to move the ball away from where the attack was going to take the Free Hit (an 'oh so sorry' 'accidental' kick or hit). If these fouls by the defense happen outside the attacking 23 meter area, blow the whistle and card the player.

If the defense does this within the attacking 23 meter area but outside the circle, blow the whistle, signal Penalty Corner and card the player. Regardless of the location on the competition surface, give the appropriate penalty and card the player who knocked away the ball or influenced play before the attack moved the ball 5 meters.

NOTE: *As this tactic is done to delay the attack, umpires can typically card the defender without having to wait for the next time the defender's team has a dead ball possession. Play is already stalled waiting for attacking team to go get the ball and bring it back to the area of the foul. The umpire should be careful not to actually help the defending team by stopping the game to card one of the defenders but, chances are, the defense has already accomplished that goal.*

DEFENSIVE FOUL ON A PENALTY CORNER

Typically, the only dead-ball foul on a Penalty Corner is when the defender breaks early into the circle before the attack has inserted the ball to restart play.

Defenders who break early into the circle before the ball is put into play on a Penalty Corner are sent up to the center-line and the team will have to defend with one less player from the back-line.

 UMPIRES: *If a defender breaks into the circle before the start of a Penalty Corner, blow your whistle loudly; reset the Penalty Corner while sending the player who broke early up to the center-line. If it happens again, send that defender to the center-line and the team will be defending with only three players. In all cases, if it is the goalkeeper who breaks early, the goalkeeper stays and another defender treks up to the center-line. The defending team continues to play short until a Penalty Corner begins legally.*

There are numerous other fouls the defense commits once the Penalty Corner has begun but they are, with the exception of one, normal playing fouls (obstruction, playing the ball with the back of the stick or their body, etc.). The one foul specific to the Penalty Corner is that a defender is not allowed to run out at the attack with a clear intent to stop a shot with their body. People call this player a suicide runner for obvious reasons. The defender demonstrates their intention by not making any legitimate attempt to play the ball with their stick.

When the ball is put into play, the defenders sent to the center-line are free to participate in the game from anywhere on the competition surface.

ATTACKING FOUL ON PENALTY CORNER

The attack player taking the insertion fouls at the start of a Penalty Corner in one of three ways. They fake on the insertion or they fail to keep one foot out of bounds prior to putting the ball in play, they use an illegal skill to put the ball into play (they lift the ball). Other attackers foul by entering the circle before the insertion takes place. In all cases, in the USA, the player who fouls must be sent to the center-line. If the inserter fouls, they must be sent to the center-line and replaced.

The attackers sent to the center-line begin from the center-line until a Penalty Corner begins legally.

When the ball is put into play, the attackers sent to the center-line are free to participate in the game from anywhere on the competition surface.

UMPIRES: You must be absolutely certain the attacker isn't faking the start of the insertion in an attempt to cause the defense to break (such as a sudden jerk without releasing the ball into the circle). This is NOT allowed.

GOALKEEPER FOULS ON A PENALTY STROKE

Prior to the execution of a Penalty Stroke, the goalkeeper might get nervous and ask that it be interrupted after appearing to be or even having said he or she was ready.

[NFHS (11.2.4): The goalkeeper and attacker must be asked if they are ready, and the goalkeeper must be asked first. Lack of a verbal response is considered an affirmative response.]

This is both understandable because of the significance of the moment and a tactic employed by some goalkeepers trying to unnerve the attacker. Umpires don't really care which it is.

This kind of tiresome behavior doesn't typically happen and, personally, I've only had to deal with it once in 45 years of officiating. In men's games, it used to be commonplace for the goalkeeper to approach the attacker, or vice versa, for a bit of a staring contest. I recommend carding either player (or both) who moved past his mark toward the other. Umpires can further caution the replacement that if it happens again, the player will be red carded. No one in his right mind will test this warning and, if one does, he isn't someone who should be in the game anyway!

NOTE: If a car backfires, a baby screams, an eagle lands on the goalkeeper's head, etc., it is okay for the goalkeeper to delay a second time. If the goalkeeper fouls AND keeps the attacker's shot from going into the goal, the Penalty Stroke is retaken. (It is commonplace in men's games for the goalkeeper to leave the line before the shot—and just as common for the attacker to score anyway.) If the goalkeeper unnecessarily delays the Penalty Stroke from being taken, the goalkeeper shall be carded.

ATTACKER FOUL ON A PENALTY STROKE

Prior to the execution of a Penalty Stroke, the attacker might get nervous and ask that it be interrupted after having appeared to be or say that he or she was ready (verbally stating readiness is not required). This is both understandable because of the significance of the moment and a tactic employed by some attackers trying to unnerve the goalkeeper. We don't really care which it is. When the attacker asks for a delay after indicating that he or she is ready, it better be for a good reason or treated as misconduct.

NOTE: If a car backfires, a baby screams, an alien tries to abduct the attacker, etc., it is okay for the attacker to delay a second time or for the umpire to ask the players to relax and reset the Penalty Stroke. But, if the attacker unnecessarily delays the Penalty Stroke from being taken, the Penalty Stroke is over.

Relationship of Location and Intent to Penalties

In real estate, there are three important variables impacting a property's value that are completely out of the control of the seller. They are:

1. Location

2. Location

3. Location

In hockey, there are three different variables impacting the type of possession a team will get in the event that an opponent fouls. The mantra isn't, *"Location. Location. Location."* It is:

1. Location

2. Intent

3. Lost Opportunity

LOCATION

A foul by the defense 48 feet 2 inches away from the goal-line (just outside the circle) might mean that the umpire is going to award a Penalty Corner to the attackers. Or, it might only be that the attack is awarded a Free Hit. And, if the exact same foul takes place just 2 inches closer to the goal-line it could mean that the umpire will be showing the signal for a Penalty Stroke. So, the location of a foul is very important.

INTENT

Overlaid on location is intent. Some will tell umpires that it isn't the umpire's job to judge intent; that umpires should only judge results. If that were the case, the *Rules of Hockey* would not use this language in Rule 9.9:

> *9.9 Players must not intentionally raise the ball from a hit except for a shot at goal.*

There are many other examples in the book where umpires are told to judge intent (nearly 20), so, please, let's stop saying umpires shouldn't judge a player's intent. In fact, umpires do need to judge the intent of a fouling player to determine how severe a penalty to apply.

What is fair to say is that if the player does X, even if the intent is not clear, then the result can be used.

A Free Hit is awarded to the attack when an attacker is unintentionally fouled by a defender outside the circle but within the attacking 23 meter area. However, an intentional foul by a defender outside the circle but within the attacking 23 meter area is penalized with a Penalty Corner.

A Penalty Corner is awarded to the attack when an attacker is unintentionally fouled by a defender inside the circle. However, an intentional foul by a defender inside the circle is penalized with a Penalty Stroke.

NOTE: In judging intent we are not asked to read minds. We judge the action. Was the action an intentional action? For example, did the defender hold her stick in such a way that in swinging at the ball the back of the stick would hit the ball? If so, the action is intentional. If, instead, the defender tripped and fell and while doing so the back of her stick happened to hit the ball, the action was not intentional. More below in the section labeled, "Judging Intentional and Unintentional Fouls".

Judging Intentional and Unintentional Fouls

After location the most important thing that dictates whether and/or how a team will be penalized is intent. One can believe that hardly anyone ever intends to foul but many an intentional action results in a foul. If the goalkeeper kicks the ball to clear it out of the circle and instead the ball smashes into the back of an attacker's stick, THAT was an unintentional foul by the attack. It's still a foul but it was unintentional.

If, however, a defender swings his or her stick wildly and it smashes into the stick of an attacker, THAT was an intentional action and, therefore, an intentional foul. It does NOT matter that the defender will likely say, *"But umpire! I was going for the ball. I didn't mean to do it!"*

At varsity high school, college, and top level hockey, umpires are to judge most actions to be intentional.

Judging what is intentional and what's unintentional is a very interesting part of the hockey umpire's job.

A player who is attempting to do something skillful and legal is a player who is IN SKILL. When an attacker is IN SKILL and a defender is IN SKILL, that's great hockey! In some cases there might even be one or more small fouls when two IN SKILL opponents are battling for the ball. Umpires do NOT have to stop two athletes who are in a contest for possession just because one or the other, during the execution of a legal skill, commits a slight error. Sticks may click and clack, an absolutely brief moment of obstruction may occur, the ball may touch the toe of one of the combatants but there is no need to whistle if the battle is fair and the athletes are making progress toward attaining possession. If no progress is being made, sure, umpires should go ahead and pick a foul—whistle and clean up the play.

When one player is IN SKILL and the opponent isn't, umpires judge the action by the opponent as intentional.

IN SKILL BUT CLUMSY: If a goalkeeper is playing legally, he or she might slip and fall on the ball. That is an accidental foul. If the goalkeeper STAYS on the ball, THAT is intentional and if there are attackers within playing distance, that's a Penalty Stroke. If the goalkeeper tries but fails to get off of the ball, we have a Penalty Corner. It was just an accidental obstruction like those caused by other defenders. However, even if this fall was accidental, if the goalkeeper's obstruction is, basically, right in front of an otherwise open goal AND there is at least one attacker there who, because of the goalkeeper's obstruction, can't bang the ball into the goal, a Penalty Stroke might be called.

Words on Whistle Timing: If the umpire waits, this falling and unsuccessful-at-getting-up goalkeeper will no doubt leave the umpire with no choice but to call a Penalty Stroke. However, if at the instant the goalkeeper falls on the ball a Penalty Corner is awarded for the simple obstruction, in most cases the correct award will have been made. We all want the attack to score goals, not be given Penalty Strokes. Keep in mind, a Penalty Stroke is a major penalty for a major foul—not the attacking team's reward for the opponent having a clumsy goalkeeper.

If a goalkeeper leaps across the goal in order to cover up the ball before an attacker reaches it, THAT is not only incredibly athletic and amazing, it is completely illegal and clearly intentional. Umpires would have to award a Penalty Stroke.

NOT IN SKILL: If a defender standing in the circle reaches for and stops a ball with the back of his or her stick, clearly the action (reaching with the stick) by the defender was intentional. Reaching for and stopping the ball with the back of the stick is NOT a legal skill. Regardless of the defender's, *"But, I didn't mean to do it,"* sincerity, the foul was intentional and the location of the ball (in the circle) when the foul occurred means that the foul will be penalized with a Penalty Stroke.

> *SCENARIO #1:* A defender swings his or her stick from his or her hip at the ball being dribbled by an attacker inside the circle toward goal and the defender hits the attacker's stick above the ball—the attack loses possession and a reasonable opportunity to shoot.

SCENARIO #2: A defender swings his or her stick along the ground (like a sweep hit) at the ball being dribbled by an attacker inside the circle toward goal and the defender hits the attacker's stick at the height of the ball (i.e. at ground level)—the attack loses possession and a reasonable opportunity to shoot.

In which scenario did the defender foul?

In the first scenario, the answer is clear—the defender fouled and, despite the, *"I didn't mean to do it,"* pleas from the defender, umpires must judge the foul to be intentional and award a Penalty Stroke. The defender moved his or her stick and hit the attacker's stick well above the ball.

In the second scenario, the answer is not clear. The defender whacked the attacker's stick, right? Well, that's true but, is it a foul. The defender's stick was at ball level the entire time. There couldn't be stick contact if the attacker's stick was still in possession of the ball—the defender's stick would have hit the ball. Obviously, then, either the attacker was obstructing the defender's stick from getting to the ball or the attacker had sent the ball ahead and the defender's strike is obstructing the attacker from getting to the ball. It all depends on where the ball is—out in front of the attacker and how far away or 'behind' the attacker's stick. Regardless, many will be expecting that the umpire is going to make a call simply because they heard the sticks clack.

We talk about umpires needing courage to make big calls. Too many people interpret that to mean that a courageous umpire will call a Penalty Stroke or issue a Red Card—as if a Penalty Stroke and a Red Card are the only measures of courage. Under the circumstances described, the courageous umpire may well be the one who awards a Free Hit to the defense in the face of pressure to make the 'big call' based on the sound of two sticks clashing together. If the attacker's stick was obstructing the defender from reaching the ball, that he or she was clearly trying to reach, the only call to make is Free Hit to the defense.

 UMPIRES: Make your decision based on what you see, not what you hear. You can be deaf to officiate hockey. You can't be blind.

The only other possible award in the situation described would be a Penalty Corner. In awarding the Penalty Corner the umpire would have to say that the attacker was IN SKILL (and not obstructing) and despite the defender's IN SKILL swing at the ball, the attacker's stick was hit and that contact kept the attacker from gaining/regaining possession. And, by possession I mean possession with the same type of potential they had before the stick contact. Having said that, if this were a breach by the defense, the description doesn't suggest a major foul but a simple, though noisy, stick obstruction.

It is situations like the second scenario that makes having an umpire's careful concentration so important.

SCENARIO #3: Umpire sees a defender slip in the mud and fall. On his or her way to the ground, the defender's stick smashes into the stick of an attacker who is dribbling inside the circle toward the goal. Was the defender's foul intentional?

In response to that question we have to say that we can only judge the actions that the defender took intentionally (none) and the outcome of those actions (a foul). Clearly, the defender was

NOT in skill and there was a foul, but it was not an intentional foul.

The attack in the third scenario would be awarded a Penalty Stroke, right? By this point in your reading, you should know enough to be saying, *"It depends on whether the defender's unintentional foul stopped what would have been a sure goal."*

Intentional Fouls Inside the Attacking 23 Meter Area

A Penalty Corner is awarded to the attack for intentional fouls by the defense inside the attacking 23 meter area. Many teenage players do not seem to have been taught this by their coaches (many coaches don't seem to know this basic rule either). I say this in such a cavalier, know-it-all way because I haven't once called a Penalty Corner for an intentional foul inside the attacking 23 meter area and not heard coaches and players express surprise and say, *"But [the foul] was outside the circle."*

This, by the way, is also a measure of how poorly umpires are performing on these calls. It has been my experience that in at least one game in two, a defender fouls intentionally inside the attacking 23 meter area and yet the umpires only award a Free Hit to the attack. If every umpire awarded a Penalty Corner under these circumstances, it wouldn't be possible for so many players and coaches to be surprised when a Penalty Corner is called for a foul outside the circle.

NOTE: There is no secondary signal for 'it was an intentional foul inside the 23 but outside the circle' and short of the potential for holding a rules lesson for every such breach, umpires are rather limited with what they should do when a coach doesn't understand why a Penalty Corner is being called for a foul outside the circle that happens inside attacking 23 meter area.

Intentional Fouls Inside the Circle

A Penalty Stroke is awarded to the attack for intentional fouls by the defense inside the circle. While most coaches will understand that this can happen, many often don't understand why it should be a Penalty Stroke and not just a Penalty Corner. In fact, one might hear a person call out, *"How can it be a penalty stroke if the goalkeeper isn't sitting on the ball?"* They might be equally likely to call out, *"That has to be a penalty stroke the goalkeeper sat on the ball!"* These comments identify someone who only has an elementary knowledge of the rules.

 UMPIRES: In the USA, if a coach is asking those questions in a disrespectful manner, you have to card the coach. If the coach wasn't being disrespectful, you can consider asking the coach to, "Please send any questions you have through your captain."

EXAMPLES OF INTENTIONAL AND UNINTENTIONAL FOULS

- A defender is running across the competition surface. An attacker hits the ball. The defender does not change pace, or move his or her feet in any way that changes a normal running stride. The ball strikes the defender's foot and bounces to the defender's teammate. This was NOT intentional. RULING: The defender's foul was an accident but a pass was made without using the flat side of the stick. The appropriate penalty is applied based on the location on the field (anywhere and everywhere outside the circle, it's a Free Hit for attack; inside the circle, it's a Penalty Corner).

- A defender is running across the competition surface. An attacker hits the ball. The defender reaches for the ball with his or her foot, the foot stops or deflects the ball and the attacker's pass is not completed. This was an intentional foul. RULING: The defender should be carded and an appropriate penalty applied based on the location on the field (outside the attacking 23 meter area equals a Free Hit to the attack; inside the attacking 23 meter area equals a Penalty Corner; inside the circle equals a Penalty Stroke). The defender protests saying, *"But I didn't mean to foul."* The coach asks the umpire, *"How can you give my player a card for that? They didn't mean to do it."* Umpires should apply appropriate card if questions continue or turn into complaints.

- An attacker breaks past a defender. The defender whirls around and attempts to tackle. The defender's stick hits the attacker's stick just outside the circle, spoiling the attack. RULING: The defender's foul was desperate and intentional. An intentional foul outside the circle but inside the attacking 23 meter area is penalized with a Penalty Corner and the defender should be carded. Had the foul happened inside the circle, it would be a Penalty Stroke and the defender should be carded. Had the foul happened outside the attacking 23 meter area, the attack would be awarded a Free Hit and the defender should be carded. The defender protests saying, *"But I didn't mean to foul."* The coach asks the umpire, *"How can you give my player a card for that? They didn't mean to do it."* Umpires should apply appropriate card if questions continue or turn into complaints.

- A defender intercepts a ball that an attacker just hit from the center-line. The defender with the ball retreats slightly and turns to the right and looks like he or she will hit the ball to a teammate standing by the far side-line. The defender strikes that ball and the ball goes over the back-line. RULING: When a defender hits the ball over the back-line, a Penalty Corner is awarded. If the umpire judges that the ground changed the direction of the ball they would award the attack a Free Hit from the 23-meter line. It is also possible that the athlete could completely botch the hit (for example when the player's swing hits the ground first and the direction the ball took was clearly not the intention of the hitter or if it were a pass to a teammate who fell on his or her way to receive the pass). However, umpires are not mind readers. If a player hits the ball over the back-line that their team is defending and there was no demonstrable outside interference, a Penalty Corner is awarded. The defender protests saying, *"But I didn't mean to foul."* The coach asks the umpire, *"How can you give my player a card for that? They didn't mean to do it."* Umpires should apply appropriate card if questions continue or turn into complaints.

- Little kids, beginners, seem to have magical powers. They can actually swing to hit the ball up the competition surface, touching the ball but— miraculously—the ball rockets across the back-line. Umpires should use common sense. At the varsity level, umpires judge results of actions to be intentional (a varsity player who hits the ball, meant to hit it where it went). At lower levels, umpires have more leeway to judging results to be accidental and in the example just described the umpire should award the attack a Free Hit from the 23-meter line instead of a Penalty Corner.

- An attacker dribbles down the side-line on his right toward a scoring opportunity. When he or she gets about ten meters from the back-line, the attacker hits the ball into the circle. A defender running into the circle reaches with his or her stick to stop the ball as it enters the circle. The defender did not turn his stick over so that the flat side or edges of the stick would block the path of the ball. The ball strikes the back of the defender's stick and deflects over the back-line. RULING: The defender's foul is intentional and within the circle so the umpire awards a Penalty Stroke. The defender protests saying, *"But I didn't mean to foul."* The coach asks the umpire, *"How can you give my player a card for that? They didn't mean to do it."* Umpires should apply appropriate card if questions continue or turn into complaints.

- An attacker dribbles down the side-line on her right toward a scoring opportunity. When he or she gets about ten meters from the back-line, the attacker crosses the ball into the circle. The ball strikes the foot of a defender who was sprinting to catch up with the attacker. The defender did not reach for the ball with her foot but the ball had entered the circle and the defender's contact with the ball kept it from reaching an attacker in the center of the circle. RULING: The defender's foul is unintentional and within the circle. The current practice is to award a Penalty Corner. The defender protests saying, *"But I didn't mean to foul."* The coach asks the umpire, *"How can you give my player a card for that? They didn't mean to do it."* Umpires should apply appropriate card if questions continue or turn into complaints.

- A defender is running across the competition surface. An attacker is dribbling the ball. The defender doesn't look like he or she is preparing to tackle. The defender does not change his or her pace or move his or her feet in any way that changes his or her run. The defender plows into the attacker. RULING: The defender's foul was not only intentional it was flagrant misconduct. Red Card! If the contact happened inside the circle, it's also a Penalty Stroke. If the contact happened inside the 23 but outside the circle, it's a Penalty Corner and a Red Card. Anyplace else, possession to the attack with a Free Hit and a Red Card.

[NFHS (12.1.PENALTIES.d): Whenever there is a flagrant red card issued to a coach, a Penalty Stroke is also awarded. It is possible for a red card to be given when the foul is not considered flagrant.]

Non-Foul Example That, In The End, Connects Many Dots

QUESTION: **An attacker stands 15-yards away from the goal line, directly in front of the goal, and takes a shot. It is a horrible shot. It isn't going anywhere near the goal and will cross the back-line 10-yards away from the goal post. The ball hits a defender's foot, deflects towards the goal but continues across the back-line. Is there a foul?**

ANSWER: **No. There was no foul. The ball was last touched by a defender but the defender did not foul.**

QUESTION: **Why not? It hit the defender's foot!**

ANSWER: **The ball, coming in contact with a foot, is not a foul. Playing the ball with your foot to the disadvantage of your opponent, now THAT is a foul. Fouls occur only when the offending team disadvantages their opponent or when dangerous play occurs.**

WHAT'S THE RULING? The result would be a Free Hit from the 23-meter line for the attack because the ball was last touched by the defense before crossing the back-line. Possession is given to the attacking team. Had the defense intentionally played the ball across the back-line, play would restart with a Penalty Corner.

In this case, the ball was going out-of-bounds, the defender did nothing to change that, and the defender's team wasn't given an advantage by the contact. Everyone on/for the attacking team will shout, *"Foot!"* Umpires should just continue to show the signal for the attack to take a Free Hit from the 23-meter line and maybe say, *"No advantage."*

Did the ball go out of bounds? Yes. Who touched it last? The defense. Therefore, the attackers might complain more (strike one), *"Why isn't that a penalty corner?"* Umpires should say something like, *"Come on. It was already on the way out. Let's go please."* If there is more complaining (strike two), the umpire should give an emphatic re-delivery of the arm signal for a Corner and sternly say, *"No more. Take your hit."* That will almost always silence any further discussion. It demonstrates that the umpire has heard enough. If there are MORE complaints (strike three), the umpire should sound his or her whistle and reverse possession awarding the ball to the opponents with a Free Hit near the side-line. Generally, that will be the end to the issue as the opponents are eager to play on and the dispossessed team will need to focus their attention on defending against the play. Should the commentary continue, the attack's captain will surely be carded.

[NFHS/NCAA: In NFHS (12.1.PENALTIES.d) and NCAA games, if someone from the bench area needs to be carded, the card is to be issued to the head coach and potentially another person whose misconduct is being addressed.]

LOST OPPORTUNITY

One more factor that is used in the final disposition of a penalty is opportunity lost. A defender that intentionally prevents an attacker from reaching the ball in the circle should, in 99% of the cases, be penalized with a Penalty Stroke being awarded to the attack. However, if this 'activity' takes place a yard from the back-line almost outside the circle, it might—unless the foul is particularly ugly—be more reasonable to signal Penalty Corner because the scoring opportunity of having the ball in that position does not come close to the scoring opportunity provided by a Penalty Stroke. If this same action happened in front of the goal, the opportunity lost (a score) due to the intentional obstruction certainly could change the outcome of the game and umpires would, without any uncertainty, award a Penalty Stroke.

With an understanding of why umpires give penalties, would it really be fair to give the attack a Penalty Corner because they hit wide of the goal but their shot happened to hit the foot of a defender on the way out?

The only thing that happened in the situation described above was that the defender slowed the ball's exit from the competition surface—possibly giving that poorly skilled attacker another shot at the goal. The attacker gave away his or her attacking advantage when he or she hit the ball wide of the target. It would be unfair to reward that pitiful effort with an attacking advantage inherent in the Penalty Corner.

Obstruction

Photograph by Ned Dawson

Hockey is fairly unique in sports because it does not let a player in possession of the ball use his or her body (or stick) to block an opponent from the ball. Doing so is called obstruction and obstruction is against the rules.

A popular rumor is that the rule governing obstruction hasn't changed for ages and that just the interpretation changed radically. Actually, the rule has changed allowing the players more flexibility with their possession skills.

In the old days, a player with the ball who turned his or her back to a defender—even when the defender could not possibly reach the ball—would lose possession for committing obstruction. Now, it is much more likely that an attacker with the ball would have to forcibly keep the defender at bay with his or her body before some umpires call an obstruction.

NOTE: Sadly, there are still some umpires around who will call a player for obstruction even though the person supposedly being obstructed can't possibly reach the ball. I call these "positional" or "visual" obstructions. These umpires are in need of coaching.

In order for there to be obstruction three things—what I've dubbed the three R's of obstruction—must ALL be occurring at the same time.

1. REACHING: The player who is being obstructed must be trying to reach the ball

2. REACHABLE: The player who is being obstructed must be close enough to reach the ball

3. REJECTED (Illegally): The player with the ball, or his or her teammate, must be actively using her stick or body to impede the player who is being obstructed from reaching the ball (we're not talking about turning ones back to the player who is 'supposedly' being obstructed but someone who turns his or her back AND backs into the player who is 'actually' being obstructed)

The umpire has to be sure that ALL THREE of these elements are present before he or she calls obstruction. Just because one is there (and often one is there) does not an obstruction make.

When an attacker does what's called a Y-dodge, they dispossess themselves by sending the ball to the right of a defender, or through the defender's legs, and then they run away from the path of the ball and around the defender to the left. These attackers, who often send the ball so far away they have to sprint just to try and regain possession, are wrongly rewarded with an obstruction call for one or two of the following reasons:

1. The attacker could no longer reach the ball (no obstruction)

2. The defender wasn't actively trying to impede the attackers path to the ball (no obstruction)

And, remember, if any one of the three conditions for obstruction are missing, there is no obstruction.

Chances are, relative to where we are as a hockey culture, if a whole bunch of people are complaining that the umpire is not calling obstruction, they're probably watching a good umpire who actually knows that all three requirements for obstruction must be present AT THE SAME TIME in order for obstruction to exist.

NOTE: If the conditions for obstruction appear to exist but the player who is 'supposedly' being obstructed raises his or her hand as if to say, "Hey. Umpire. Look! I'm being obstructed," the umpire may well have decided that the player is not trying to play the ball and so, one of the requirements for obstruction is not taking place so obstruction cannot be called.

It has been stressed to the officiating community NOT to 'give' an attacker an obstruction call when:

1. The attacker decides to dispossess himself or herself of the ball (puts it beyond his or her reach)

2. The attacker decides to run away from the path of the ball (think, Y-dodge)

Similarly, umpires should not interfere with the flow of the game if:

1. The attacker is dribbling away from the defender and the defender is chasing the attacker very closely—even when

the defender becomes frustrated by the attacker's evasive actions (i.e. the attacker's cool dribbling)

2. The defender is not attempting to play the ball when the attacker would otherwise be obstructing

OBSTRUCTION SCENARIOS (Part I)

In which, if any, of the following six situations does it appear that the whistle should be blown and possession be given to the team in white because the team in black is obstructing?

I've provided the answers at the end of this section.

1.   2.   3.

4.   5.   6.

OBSTRUCTION SCENARIOS (Part II)

Below are three more obstruction scenarios to test your judgment about how to call obstruction.

a. There are three players in the following illustration, one from the black-footed team, two from the white-footed team. The black-footed team has possession. The arrow indicates the direction and distance with which the member of the black-footed team has played the ball. The two members of the white-footed team are about three meters away from each other. Does it appear that in either of these situations that the whistle should probably be blown and possession be given to the black-footed team because the white-footed team is obstructing?

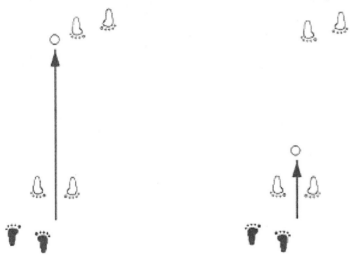

b. In the following scenario there is only one player from each team in the illustration. The black-footed player has possession. The arrow indicates the direction and distance with which the member of the black-footed team has played the ball. The black foot prints show the path to the right taken by the black-footed player after placing the ball to the right of the opponent from the white-footed team. Is this obstruction?

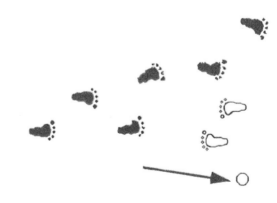

c. There is only one player from each team in this final illustration regarding obstruction. The black-footed team has possession. The white-footed team is defending the nearest goal. The black-footed player had dribbled in along the back-line from the left outside position. As the black-footed player approached the circle, he or she turns up the competition surface and puts the ball just behind the player from the white-footed team (as indicated by the length of the arrow). Just as quickly as the ball is put between the feet of the white-footed defender, the white-footed player pivots and dribbles the ball away from the back-line and the black-footed player who is rushing after the ball. The black-footed player continues to follow the white-footed player trying to get the ball. Clearly, the white-footed player's body is between the black-footed player and the ball. Is this obstruction?

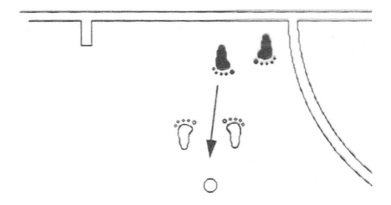

Answers
Part I –   Only drawings 4 and 5 show possible obstructions
Part IIa – Only the illustration on the right shows a possible obstruction
Part IIb – No obstruction. The attacker dispossessed him or herself of the ball and then ran away from the path of the ball
Part IIc – No obstruction. The attacker dispossessed him or herself of the ball and then defender turned around, took the ball and ran away

Danger and Dangerous Play

When should an umpire call something dangerous? If what just happened makes you gasp, that's a good indication it was dangerous. Having said that, umpire do NOT penalize incredible goals as being dangerous just because the shots make people gasp. Remember, the goal is seven feet tall (a shot can be successful if it is 6'11" high) and the goalkeeper has a ton of equipment on that the other players don't, so almost no shot is going to be considered dangerous for the completely equipped goalkeeper.

A legal shot on the goalkeeper is, in almost all cases, a legal shot against anyone who decides to stand where, arguably, only a goalkeeper ought to!

That said, no player should ever force another player to defend themselves against a ball raised to any height. Further, a shooter must shoot at the goal and not at a defender positioned between the shooter and the goal. A shot raised high *at* a defender demonstrates a lack of consideration for the safety of others and might be considered deliberate endangerment—it is difficult to tell the difference. It cannot be declared 'not legitimate' for a defender to position themselves to defend the goal between a shooter and the goal if we also agree that a player can take up any position on the field. No position on the pitch is, in and of itself, against the rules. If, however, an umpire judges that a field player has positioned themselves for the sole purpose of playing the ball with their body, the player can be penalized.

JUDGING DANGER

There is much that can be said with regard to judging whether a play is dangerous or not. Certainly one player pushing another is unacceptable and can also be dangerous—especially if a player is pushed to the ground—but not every push is dangerous. Shoving, most of us would agree, is more dangerous than leaning into an opponent and a punch is much more dangerous than a shove. That escalation of what is dangerous is easy.

What about hits that rise into the air or a flick or scoop (the latter are two skills that intentionally lift the ball) that pass close to an opponent? When do flicks, scoops, and raised hits become dangerous? Is it the speed of the ball, the proximity of the ball to the opponent's upper body, the proximity of the opponent to the start of the play, or should umpires only consider how close the ball is to an opponent's head?

Would a player's grandmother who has never seen a hockey game judge a rising hit's dangerousness the same way that a top international player would? If you were umpiring, would your judgment be somewhere between the grandmother's and that of the international's? What if you had to officiate a game between a bunch of first graders or the gold medal game in the next Olympics? Whichever level it is, would fans watching the game feel that the umpires were calling danger the same way? Should both umpires on a game, whatever the level of the competition, call danger the same way?

How can we work to get all umpires calling danger in a similar fashion, consistently at both ends of the competition surface and from one game to the next?

Leonardo da Vinci's Vitruvian Man (ca. 1487)

Leonardo da Vinci's Vitruvian Man (1487) provides a visual of what I call the player's "jumping jack space". When an opponent violates this space with his or her stick or causes the ball to fly through it, an umpire is free to make an assessment about whether the play was dangerous. A ball (or an opponent's stick) that is outside the "jumping jack space" CANNOT be considered dangerous.

Of course, not every ball or stick sent into an opponent's jumping jack space is dangerous. Could the ball, at the speed it is traveling, cause injury? Was the ball put up from less than 5 meters away? Did the stick nearly hit the player in the head?

It is reasonable to use skill level to refine what should be considered dangerous. The following series highlights that as skill increases—from a novice to a member of a national team—the space decreases in which a ball traveling at an injurious velocity should warrant the umpire's whistle.

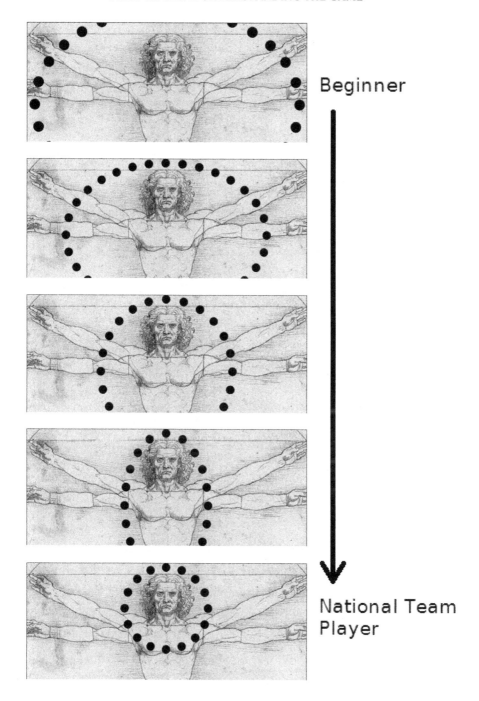

Beginner

National Team Player

Another important body marker used in judging danger is a player's knees.

Above the knee = danger is a consideration.

Below the knee = danger is rarely a consideration.

If a ball is lifted or hit into an opponent's body from a short distance away and hits the player above his or her knees, the play is likely to be ruled dangerous. Generally, if the player is hit below the knees the play is not considered dangerous.

ACTIVITY: Do a jumping jack. Do your hands reach below your knees?

If, however, an opponent hits the ball blindly or smashes it at a player with reckless abandon, the play can be considered dangerous even if it strikes the player in the feet or shins (i.e. below the knees).

It used to be but it is no longer considered dangerous to carefully bat a raised ball forward into the goal. This doesn't mean the attacker gets to swing away at the ball like Babe Ruth swinging for the fences (unless the goal is empty and no one is near the attacker). Because this action, called batting, used to be specifically forbidden, even the safest execution of this shot will cause some (old) people to shout, *"You can't bat the ball in the air!"* But, the ball can be batted!

UMPIRES: If a coach says that, it is a negative public comment and must be carded.

During a situation in which there is dangerous play, if the umpire is holding the whistle—mentally—for advantage and the team that should get the ball does get the ball, umpires might still want to card the dangerous player at the next change of possession.

A player for the Red team has the ball just inside the 23 meter area and sees that a teammate is standing open at the top of the circle. As a defender from the Blue team rushes up to pressure the ball handler, the Red player turns and runs away from Blue team defender. Knowing that his or her teammate is waiting at the top of the circle, without turning the Red team's attacker smashes the ball backwards in an attempt to pass the ball to his or her teammate. The ball meets the Blue defender's feet, however, and stalls the play. What is the color of the uniform worn by the players who get the ball after the umpire's whistle, Blue or Red?(Answer in second bullet below.)

Here are some incidents when the umpire should always whistle to stop dangerous behavior or actions that might lead to danger (unless the umpire is holding for advantage):

- An attacker in close quarters with a defender swings to hit the ball and misses AND the direction of the follow through is towards the body of the defender. The miss demonstrates that the player is clearly out of control. Such a miss, however, is NOT dangerous when restarting play when no opponent is within 5 meters of the player who swings and misses.

A player hits the ball blindly into an opponent. (This is what happened in the example above involving the attacker with a teammate standing open at the top of the circle. I hope you answered Blue.)

- A player lifts his or her stick over an opponent's head (you'll typically see this done by an attacker during a dodge). This is specifically illegal and must be whistled as dangerous and most often carded.

Umpires do NOT penalize players for actions taken to protect themselves from danger (for example, if while protecting him or herself the ball hits the back of their stick). Umpires also do NOT penalize players for their strength and power! Hitting a ball really hard is not, in and of itself, dangerous.

 UMPIRES: It is generally, though not always, the case that when an attacker hits the ball and the ball hits the defender below the knee that we blame the defender. Similarly, if the ball hits a defender above the knee, we blame the attacker. On Penalty Corners, if the attacker shoots into the air and the ball strikes the Flyer (the defender rushing out first to defend the attacker's shot) above the knee, you award possession to the Flyer's team. That said, the Flyer must not, for the sole purpose of illegally blocking a shot, run into the path of the attacker's shot.

QUESTION: **When a Blue team player hits the ball within a few inches of a player's head, when is that not dangerous?**

ANSWER: **If the other player is also on the Blue team. A player's dangerous action is not considered dangerous unless it endangers an opponent.**

Aerials

When there is an aerial, umpires are asked to assess whether the ball went up safely and if the ball will fall into an open space or if it is clear who the initial receiver is – which isn't to say that the ball is clearly going to the lifter's teammate but, whether the umpire can tell who will get the ball first.

If the ball isn't going to land in open space and the umpire cannot instantly tell who will get the ball first, the umpire should immediately whistle – while the ball is still in the air – and give a Free Hit to the opponent in the space that the ball is going to return to the competition surface.

When it is clear who the initial receiver is, it should also be clear to all the players. All the other players must allow the initial receiver to get the ball on the ground and in control before they are allowed to challenge for possession. Again, the initial receiver might be the teammate or an opponent of the player who lifted the ball.

1.   Did the ball leave the ground safely?

The athlete preparing to lift the ball into the air must select an open space on the competition surface from which the ball can be safely lifted. Some opponents will run into a place where an athlete is obviously preparing to throw the ball for the sole purpose of trying to make it look like the player about to put the ball into the air is playing dangerously. In fact, an opponent who runs into the space is the one who is playing dangerously.

2.   Trajectory

Having successfully lifted the ball into the air without danger, the ball must also travel through its course in the air without causing danger or leading to dangerous play. In short, the ball has to be well above everyone's head.

3. Destination

The player who throws the ball into the air must have either selected a space in which the ball will land or passed it to an obvious receiver. As soon as the ball is put into the air the umpire should determine the destination or landing zone of the ball.

If the ball is headed towards a place occupied by several players from both teams and the umpire cannot instantly determine who the initial receiver is, the umpire should blow his or her whistle during the flight of the ball. The subsequent possession, the Free Hit, is given to the opponents based on where the ball is returning to the competition surface.

If the ball is headed to an open space, then only one player may enter that space before the ball returns to the competition surface. If two opponents run into the space at the same time, it is the teammate of the player who put the ball into the air that must give up the space. If only one person from either team is in the space where the ball will come down, the player who created the aerial selected the destination safely. Some opponents will run into a place where an athlete is getting ready to receive a lofted ball for the sole purpose of trying to make it look like the aerial was dangerous. In fact, an opponent who comes into the space before the receiver has the ball on the ground and under control is the one who is playing dangerously.

4. Reception

Only one person may receive an aerial. It is dangerous for a second player to attempt to receive the ball. If one person from either team is preparing to receive the ball, then NO OTHER player can come near that player. If two opponents are in the landing area, and the ball is falling <u>between</u> them (and the umpire doesn't blow the whistle), it is accepted common practice that the teammate of the player who put the ball into the air must allow the opponent to safely receive the ball. The other player must not engage the receiver until he/she has the ball on the ground and under control. There is NO requirement for the lifter's teammate to leave the area. The teammate is like a player caught within 5 meters of a Free Hit – they simply cannot influence play.

NOTE: Good aerials tend to beat everyone. They go over everyone's head and an attacker runs on to the dropping ball and, without breaking stride, picks it up off the bounce and begins dribbling to goal.

AERIAL SCENARIOS

The team in black has possession. Should the whistle be blown in any of the following situations and should possession be given to the attack (team in black) or the defense (team in white)? If so, from where would the game be restarted, A or B? Answers below.

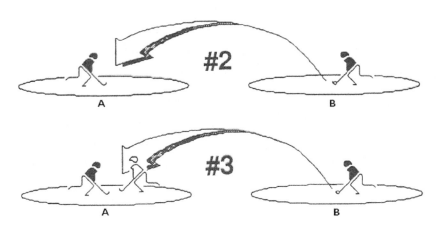

IMPORTANT: *In the third scenario, given that a player from each team is already in the destination area, the player in black on the left, MUST give the opponent an abundance of time and space in which the opponent can safely receive the ball and control it on the ground. A good way to practice making this call is to visualize the scenarios presented above. You might find it helpful to watch a soccer game, because the ball is put into the air so often, and simply pretend that you're calling a hockey game. When two or more soccer players jump up in a group to head the ball, that aerial would be a foul against the attack in hockey with a restart for the defense at the place that the ball was coming down because the receiving attacker did not give his or her opponent time and space to get the ball under control.*

Answers (where should the ball be restarted)

1 = Dangerous, restart at B (this to the defender's head!)

2 = Not dangerous, no foul, no whistle, an aerial - lifted high into the air, returning to one player - is never, in and of itself, dangerous

3 = The 'group' of players might react safely but the teammate of the player who lifted the ball, must give the opponent space and time to receive the ball onto the ground, restart at A if black doesn't back off or if the umpire has any question as to who the initial receiver will be

Shots on Goal

One of the most important things umpires have to get right when officiating is judging whether or a not a ball that's gone completely across the goal-line was shot legally. If it was, it's a, *"Gooooooooooooooooal!"*

Here are some of the questions that have to be answered "Yes," in order for a goal to be scored:

- Did the whole ball go completely across the goal-line? (If the ball breaks apart prior to crossing the goal-line, a goal is not scored and play is restarted with a bully even if all parts of the ball went across the goal-line, the 'whole' ball didn't.)

- Was the ball touched inside the circle by an attacker's stick or a defender's stick or body without leaving the circle before crossing the goal line? (The attacker's body does not have to be inside the circle.)

- Was the skill used to take the shot a hit and, if it were, was this hit the first shot on goal during a Penalty Corner? If so, the ball may not be on a path to cross the goal-line higher than 18 inches unless it was deflected by a defender or legally by an attacker.

- If the shot came on a Penalty Corner, had the ball already gone outside the circle?

After an umpire has correctly processed all of the above for a shot that raced into the upper left corner of the goal, they will probably hear someone shout from the side-line, *"Wasn't that shot dangerous?"* The umpire ought to be able to answer that question though, they don't have to answer out loud.

UMPIRES: If you think it necessary, answer by shaking your head (feigning disbelief) and re-show your goal signal.

Teenage attackers are getting better and stronger and they're demonstrating more creativity when it comes to their shooting skills. Very often this means that shots are entering the goal in the air. These shots may or may not be dangerous. Remember two things. One, we want skillful play to be rewarded (and therefore encouraged) and two, the goal is 7 feet tall.

THINK ABOUT IT: The internal height of a hockey goal is seven feet. If lifted shots were not allowed, the crossbar of a hockey goal might only be about six inches off the ground.

Judging a raised shot on goal is different than judging an aerial made in open field play. The entirety of the goalmouth is a very important LEGAL target.

So, how do umpires judge when a shot is truly dangerous?

When is a shot that hits a defending field player NOT dangerous?

If a shot is stopped by the feet or lower legs of a defending field player, then the shot is ABSOLUTELY NOT dangerous and, if it is not certain that the ball would have entered the goal (i.e., another defender, for example the goalkeeper, is behind the defender who was hit by the ball), a Penalty Corner is awarded.

Generally, if a shot is taken from more than 5 meters away from a defender who is standing in front of the shot, and it is stopped from going into the goal by the body (thighs, stomach, chest, head) of defending field player, the shot is NOT considered dangerous to the defender and a Penalty Stroke is awarded the attack. This suggests that a rock hard ball traveling at over 50 miles an hour (fairly typical for a skilled teenage girl) can't be dangerous to a defender who is more than 5 meters away.

WHEN IS A SHOT DANGEROUS?

First, almost every shot on goal should be considered legal. It is truly the exception, the rare occasion, in which we would consider a shot illegal. The one exception is when a raised shot hits or just misses a defending field player above the defender's knees, the defending field player was in extremely close proximity to the attacker, much less than 5 meters away, and the velocity of the shot was such that injury would have occurred if the defender had been struck by the ball. In that case, the shot can be considered dangerous.

If the ball didn't hit the defender, for example just missing the defender's head, some will argue that the shot was not dangerous—that instead, because no one was hit, the shot safe.

I would argue that if the attacker could place the ball that perfectly, then the attacker should have elected to put the ball even further away from the defender's head.

The rules do not make it clear what is and is not a dangerous shot. The guidance for rule 9.9 reads, *"A flick or scoop towards an opponent within 5 metres is considered dangerous."* Most people would say this must also be applied to use of a hitting action.

Later in the rules, the guidance for rule 13.3 reads, *"If a defender is within five metres of the first shot at goal during the taking of a penalty corner and is struck by the ball below the knee, another penalty corner must be awarded or if struck on or above the knee in a normal stance, the shot is judged to be dangerous and a free hit must be awarded to the defending team."*

While 13.3 is discussing shots taken during Penalty Corners, because the passage is about safety, common sense would have the same guidance applied during other shooting situations.

There are some who believe that no shot on goal can be dangerous. Such an ideology has been demonstrated empirically not to be the case through both minor and life threatening injuries.

WHAT IS THE EXCEPTION?

An attacker is not allowed to hit a ball directly at a defender who is in an established defending position and less than 5 meters away (5 yards in NFHS) from the attacker. If on the first shot during a Penalty Corner the ball hits the Flyer (the 'Flyer' is the defending field player who rushes out further than all other defenders on a Penalty Corner to stop the first shot) above the Flyer's knee while he or she is running out in a legitimate position to defend against the first shot, it is always considered a dangerous hit and a Free Hit is awarded to the defense (unless the defender was actually trying to get hit as a way of blocking the shot).

IMPORTANT: If a shot pops up and flies over everyone's head, it isn't dangerous to anyone!

The Drag Flick skill is used to take shots on goal. It is illegal to use a drag flick on Penalty Strokes, Free Hits, Corners (Long Hits), Center Pass, Hit-Ins ("16's") and Side-Ins. Due to the amount of time typically needed to perform this skill, it is almost exclusively used on Penalty Corners. It is almost never done on a grass surface but don't be surprised if you're the first to see it done! In the hands of a skilled player, the Drag Flick propels the ball to the goal at an exciting speed (remember, just because it is fast doesn't make it illegal).

If any flick is used as a first shot during a Penalty Corner and it strikes the Flyer above the knee, the shot is considered dangerous. An exception would be if the goalkeeper is the Flyer. An aerial against a goalkeeper coming out first on Penalty Corners, i.e. flying, can legally hit the goalkeeper anywhere (unless it was the first shot and the hitting action was used AND the path of the ball would have seen it cross the goal-line higher than 18 inches).

Collisions

Opponents sometimes collide during hockey games. More often than not, when a collision happens, it's because a goalkeeper and an attacker are going for a 50/50 ball. Even in the most violent of collisions, it's possible that neither player has fouled.

Hockey is a sport, collisions happen. So, two players bang into each other. They often fall to the ground and sometimes they get hurt. Most times they just get up, shake it off and keep going. In almost all cases, it sure LOOKS bad. Again, just because there is a collision doesn't mean there is a foul.

When there is a collision and one team gets an advantage as a result, that advantage was gained illegally—typically from an obstruction. The umpire gives possession to the team that was disadvantaged. When neither team is disadvantaged, no foul.

Alternately, what if there was a foul by both teams? What should the umpire do in the case of simultaneous fouls? That's sort of a trick question. In the *Rules of Hockey*, there is no such thing as simultaneous fouls. Something happened first. As mentioned earlier, in NFHS games, misconduct fouls can be considered to have occurred simultaneously (8.2.PENALTIES.3) but, the situation is considered poorly umpired if an umpire cannot decide which foul happened first.

 UMPIRES: If you're officiating when one of these collisions occurs and the ball—and play around it—is dead, blow the whistle and signal to stop the clock. Check to see if the athletes are okay and restart with a Bully. This gives everyone (including the parents and fans) a chance to calm down and feel better knowing that you've taken notice of the situation.

If play continues away from the collision, umpires should allow it to continue. If one of the athletes appears to be injured, follow the instructions in the section of this book called *When an Injury Happens.*

Two opponents running side-by-side, chasing after a loose ball, might bump into each other during their competition for the ball. Umpires watch for pushing and elbowing (even if to "find a foul" to clean up the play if the umpire feels it is too much contact) but permissible "athletic contact" and "normal bumping" is likely to occur.

A player in possession of the ball, however, who is bumped by a defender has been fouled. Sometimes this contact is purposefully subtle with the umpire's eyes lured away from the upper body where the contact will take place by an exaggerated stick tackle. A field player who collides with an opponent, forcing them off their feet, didn't only foul; they played dangerously and should be carded, with a yellow or a red.

All that said, there is no specific collision rule, the umpires must use the information they see and apply common sense.

Behavior Management Skills

"We have to make decisions in 100th of a second. If we had twice as much time, maybe we'd be right 100% of the time."

> – Steven Horgan, Director of Umpiring, USA Field Hockey

CARDING

Umpires shouldn't be afraid of using their cards and using them early in a game. Some umpires don't know when and how to use cards so they never employ them. You might even meet an old umpire who brags, *"I've been officiating for 40 years and I've never had to card a player or a coach."* Translation, *"I've been officiating badly for 40 years."*

 UMPIRES: Do NOT listen to bad umpires.

Carding is not special. It is just a fancy whistle in an umpire's pocket that must be used to record that they have seen or heard unacceptable behavior. It isn't a big deal to card an athlete or a coach—it's simply part of the game.

 UMPIRES: When you're going to card someone, you want everyone's attention because you are sending a signal to everyone involved in the game not to repeat the unacceptable behavior. Make your carding whistle LONG and LOUD, signal time-out, identify the offending athlete (point at them telling them to leave the game), and then show the card. Be sure to write the time, player's number, and type of card on your recording material.

Umpires who don't accept the idea that carding should be commonplace are the same umpires who only card in anger. They let a situation get under their skin and then, finally, a 'last straw' event takes place and the umpire explodes! They signal time-out, run over to the player to be carded, and shake the card at the player while lecturing them about this, that, and the other thing. That is the WRONG way to card and it destroys the very intention of carding. It shouts out, *"I don't know what I'm doing!"* I can promise you that you'll see that umpire someday.

Carding should be simple, fast, and professional. It should eliminate negative behavior, not cause the umpire to act in a manner that should itself be carded! Umpires should never chase after or lecture a player. Umpires are not allowed to coach and, arguably, lecturing is coaching.

Unless it is a red card, in which case the person getting the card is disqualified, carding can be thought of as a formal near-written request that the person getting the card change his or her behavior—immediately! With a red card, the umpire doesn't really care if the person changes their behavior immediately because the person who earned the red card is no longer involved with the competition.

The unofficial card is a strong whistle and the "don't do THAT again" look.

The "don't do THAT again" look is used at opportune moments during a game—perhaps when there has been stick contact on a sloppy but not particularly harsh tackle in mid-field. The umpire has blown his/her whistle loud and long and the offending athlete is looking at him/her. The umpire should reaffirm the hard whistle by expressing his/her displeasure with the player's actions by looking unhappy and moving his/her head back-and-forth as in, *"No."*

If the athlete says, *"What's that mean?"* the umpire should show them (in this example) the stick obstruction signal (perhaps exaggerated), shake their head and say, *"No more stick tackles like that."* They can express it in a friendly way and make the point.

The Cards

- The LOOK (not really a card): Loud whistle, a semi-private caution (*"Come on. No more of that."*)

- GREEN CARD: Whistle, point at player, "swipe" them out of the game, record warning, player receives a two-minute suspension

- YELLOW CARD: Whistle, point at player, "swipe" them out of the game, record warning, player receives a five-minute suspension (or longer, and at least 10 minutes if the foul was physical in nature, i.e. a push or takedown)

- RED CARD: Whistle, point at player, "swipe" them out of the game record warning, the player is disqualified

[NFHS: Umpires are required to stop time when carding a player (2.1.6,). If a player receives a Yellow Card, the player is suspended for either 5 or 10 minutes (8.2.PENALTIES.1.b). No more. No less. There are not two types of Yellow Cards for coaches – only 5 minute Yellow Cards (12.1.PENALTIES.1.b)]

 UMPIRES: Make sure the team only plays with the proper number of players during the suspension. Some teams think this is a forced substitution and don't play a player down after a carding. In fact, some youngsters are trained to go into the game if a certain player comes off. Just be mindful after a carding that the proper number of players are in the game.

CARDING MECHANICS (Players)

An athlete for the Blue team is about to restart play with a Free Hit. The athlete hits the ball and it soars into the air in a dangerous manner. The umpire awards possession to the Red team. Later in the game the Blue team gets another Free Hit and again restarts play with a hit and the ball flies into the air endangering opponents. The umpire sees that the Blue team is sorry; the umpire gives the players a look of disappointment and awards possession to the Red team. Later the Blue team gets another Free Hit, smacks the ball into the air and this time it hits one of the opponents in the chest. The umpire blows their whistle, signals Free Hit to the Red team and tells the Blue players to be more careful.

What has the umpire done to motivate the athletes to change their dangerous play? All we have is the umpire 'penalizing' the Blue team over and over again by giving possession to the Red team. Despite a stern look or words of caution from the umpire, there has been no escalation of 'punishment' and (surprise, surprise) no change in behavior.

"Insanity is doing the same thing over and over again and expecting different results." — Albert Einstein

The umpire must do something different in order to get different results—the Blue team should have been carded on the second dangerously taken Free Hit.

In the old days (way back in 2011), umpires were instructed to card players with an emphasis on stopping the game to, basically, put on a show. To demonstrate to everyone exactly what type of misconduct was being carded and who was getting the card. It was, a moment. Everything stopped, the crowd quieted down in anticipation, the player came over to the umpire, the umpire assured that the player turned to show his or her number to the table, and then, wait for it—the card!

This also provided the 'stage' for bad umpires to lecture and often belittle the athletes. It made the umpire the center of attention.

Now, with a realization that it isn't necessary to put on such a demonstration (in order to inform everyone what behavior was being carded and to let the scorekeeper know who was carded) and that it is in everyone's best interest that the hockey game is played, not stopped, the process of giving a card has changed. In short, carding is to be much less dramatic and the emphasis is on NOT stopping the game for very long at all.

NOTE: Umpires should demonstrate a very low tolerance for players hitting the ball away 'just after' a whistle. It is simply amazing how much better the athletes will get at NOT "accidentally" hitting the ball away, as if they just couldn't stop themselves before, if the umpires card a player for their 'mistake'.

MODERN CARDING

The umpire blows the whistle. He or she points (preferably with an open hand) to the player being carded, then holds up the card to be given high in the air. Any words the umpire uses, and typically none are necessary, must be limited to exactly what the issue was, *"Leave the ball alone on their free hit."* The umpire should not lecture the athlete—that's the coach's prerogative.

More important than words, the umpire has to be sure to show the appropriate secondary signal (if there is one for the incident), for example the sign for danger, in association with displaying the card.

When it is clear that the appropriate player has been identified, that player should leave the competition surface without further comment or interaction with the umpire. At the moment the carded athlete is heading off the field, time should be restarted. The suspended player has the responsibility to leave the field without continuing to influence play. If the suspended player does influence play while leaving the field, another, more severe card should be given.

If a yellow card is given, the umpire must indicate to the table how long the athlete's suspension is to last.

 UMPIRES: Typically you only card the player when their team has possession. In the case described above with the Blue team hitting the ball away, go ahead and issue the card. Although the ball will be given to the Red team, neither team has possession because the ball was hit away and it will probably take a little time before play can be restarted. The card can be given in that moment.

At the time of the carding the umpire should CALMLY reach into their pocket and CALMLY pull out the card the player (or coach) has earned. One reason the cards are different shapes is so the umpire can sort through the cards while they're out-of-view and only bring out the card that is needed. In short, the umpire doesn't have to pull out all their cards.

Umpires should not carry the cards attached to each other. If they do, when they pull the cards out of their pocket and hold them overhead (see photo below) it might be hard to discern exactly which card was being applied and, we really don't want to have to spend time figuring out which card was being shown. That would stall the restart of the game.

UMPIRES: Do NOT hold up all your cards at the same time. It is important that people see THE card that is being issued, not that you have all your cards.

Present yourself with the highest level of professionalism when a player or coach earns a card by only showing one card. Avoid questions about which card was earned by only removing one card from your pocket. If your warning cards are attached to each other, detach them!

Write down the carding information on the recording materials that you are required by rule to carry with you. You should record color of card and the number and team of the player being carded. I do this by drawing the shape of the card around the player's number on my recording materials. You might also note the time of card and, if a yellow card, minutes suspended.

In a perfect world the player being carded would say, *"I'm sorry. I shouldn't have done that. It won't happen again,"* and <u>then</u> they might ask, *"What did I do?"* In the real world, however, the athlete being carded typically says that they don't understand why they're being carded – even if the umpire tells them.

It doesn't matter. The carded athlete doesn't have to say anything and, umpires do not have to call the athlete over for a chat. Umpires are presenting the card and showing or telling the athlete the action for which they are being carded. The player is being carded for that action. If the player responds to the carding by speaking rudely or acting disrespectfully, that behavior is to be penalized with a more severe card.

UMPIRES: If you do speak to a player, pretend that ALL of what you tell the player can be overheard by millions of people watching the game on television—or on a YouTube video taken with a fan's cell phone. The fact is, what you say may well end up going viral on YouTube. Your words should benefit the players, the coaches, the fans—everyone within hearing distance (and those who hear a recording of what you say). You don't need to say much more than can be communicated with arm signals or brief phrases.

In the circumstance of the player repeatedly hitting the ball up dangerously umpires might say something like, *"No dangerous hits."* But, is it really necessary? Doesn't everyone already know what led to the carding?

Umpires might want to be disarming and say something like, *"This cow pasture we're playing on is killing you but I've got to penalize you for those dangerous hits. Perhaps you should push it or not hit it quite so hard. We don't want anyone to get hurt."*

In all carding situations, umpires want to look calm and more professional than at any other time during the match.

UMPIRES: Record the carding on your MatchSKIN™ (or similar) and make sure your partner has it recorded and knows what the carding was for before allowing play to continue. More information is available on MatchSKINS.com.

Some umpires 'over engineer' carding situations. They give a long speech or lecture the player. They go over to the scorer's table and give a long-winded explanation of what happened as if the 14 year-old scorekeeper is a court stenographer. The most that scorekeeper needs to be told is something like, *"Number five,*

Blue team, yellow card, 5 minutes. Got it?" Even that is silly. The scorekeeper can discern all of that all by themselves by watching the game. It is not the umpire's job to see that the carding is properly recorded by the scorekeeper.

IMPORTANT: While it is certainly important that the athlete know what color card they have earned, the umpire should NOT show the card to the athlete in a manner that might be seen as being aggressive. I've seen umpires shake the card at the player, almost like the umpire is scolding the athlete. Until the final whistle blows, the athletes are in 'warrior mode' and aggressive behavior on the part of the umpire can't help but be seen as being combative. Umpires are not there to compete with the players. In fact, umpires are there to help the players, to facilitate their competition.

Now that the game has been briefly interrupted, how does the game get going again?

CRITICAL I: Before restarting the game after a carding, the umpire must make sure the players are in position to begin playing. The umpire must make it clear which team will restart the game with possession and that they know not to put the ball into play until after the whistle to restart play. If the clock was stopped, umpires should check with the timer to make sure they're ready to begin the clock when the whistle is blown. The umpires have to get themselves into position, check with each other to be sure each is ready, and THEN the whistle is blown.

CRITICAL II: All the points made above are even more important when restarting after a timeout prior to a Penalty Corner. When the umpire blows his or her whistle to signal time in at the start of a Penalty Corner, the athletes are likely to break on the sound of the whistle unless the umpire takes steps to ensure they don't. Rather than standing in the position they'll officiate the Penalty Corner from, time should be restarted while the umpire is in front of the goal. The umpire might even ask the players to come off their starting position, have them relax while the umpire blows the whistle for the start of time THEN, after the whistle is blown, the players go about setting up the Penalty Corner. All that being said, it is almost certain that the rules will change in 2019 and the umpire will blow the whistle to indicate that it's time for the Penalty Corner to begin.

QUESTION (True or False): **A player on the Blue team hacks and pushes an attacker from behind as the attacker crosses the center-line. Without whistling, the umpire signals advantage and allows play to continue. The attack finishes with a shot that goes wide of the goal. The umpire signals for time-out and wants to card the Blue team defender who pushed and tackled improperly from behind. Unfortunately, neither umpire knows the defender's number. The umpire calls the defender's team captain over and tells the captain to bring over the player who had fouled. The captain says that he or she doesn't know who the player was. The umpire awards the card to the captain.**

ANSWER: **True. The captain is responsible for the actions of all the players on his or her team.**

Too many umpires hold carding in reserve for something really bad. By then, it's often too late to properly manage the game. A good call is a good call. Making a carding call for misconduct should happen just as early in the game and as quickly as a non-carding call is made for an inappropriate action like obstruction.

When an umpire cards, they are trying to change behavior—not only for this game but also in all games that ever follow.

Carding helps all of the umpires who will ever have the carded player (or coach) in the future. Carding builds a foundation that will advance hockey for years and years to come.

A carding call (to me) includes when umpires only use a LONG and LOUD whistle. There are some things that REQUIRE an actual card but there are other actions that can be managed in such a way that an actual card doesn't have to be given.

Umpires should not hesitate to give a card when a player has demonstrated a total disregard for the rules or the safety of their opponents.

CARDING MECHANICS (Coaches)

The word coach does not appear in the *Rules of Hockey* nor does any surrogate. The team's captain is responsible for the conduct of their teammates and, by extension, the non-playing team personnel (the coaches). Umpires in the USA, however, do have provisions for carding coaches.

In the NFHS rules, however, there is quite a bit of time spent describing what happens when a coach has been carded. This is because there is no technical table taking care of coaches who demonstrate poor sportsmanship, less than appropriate decorum or outright misconduct. Very specific penalties are applied for each level of card that is earned by an NFHS coach. Check with the latest copy of the NFHS rulebook for details.

The main, overriding difference between carding a coach in an NFHS game and any other game of hockey is that the NFHS coach's behavior can impact the game's result. If an NFHS coach gets a red card for flagrant behavior, the opponents get a Penalty Stroke (12.1.PENALTIES.d). This, in my opinion, is an unfair way that the NFHS rules allow a coach to take the outcome of the game away from the athletes.

[NFHS: While there are no player suspension for a coach's green card (12.1.PENALTIES.1.a), the team must play short for five minutes if its coach gets a yellow card, there is no 10-minute yellow card for coaches (12.1.PENALTIES.1.b). A red card causes the team to play short for the remainder of the game. If a coach's red card was for a flagrant foul, the opponent is also given a Penalty Stroke (12.1:PENALTIES.1.d).]

When a coach has earned a card, it is best that the umpire signals timeout at a stoppage of play when the offending coach's team has possession. The umpire points at the coach with their arm (open hand, palm up) and shows the card to the scorekeeper by holding it high overhead. Then, with as little break in the action as possible, the game should be continued by enforcing any necessary penalties.

If a coach is insistent on knowing why he or she has been carded, the explanation is typically either, *"Verbal misconduct,"* or *"Team area violation."* There are eight types of misconduct listed in the NFHS rule book. "Excessive coaching" was removed from that list in 2020.

I have been more specific with coaches, for example, *"It is misconduct to make negative public comments about the officiating,"* but less is more when carding. You're delivering information, not welcoming debate.

 UMPIRES: *You are not at the game to teach the coach or the players the rules of the game. You are there to enforce the current rules according to the current guidance.*

If the coach continues complaining, it is a NEW misconduct. Another word on the subject from the coach and the umpire is compelled to card the coach again with a more severe card.

If a coach questions my officiating, I might give two quick whistles (tweet-tweet), the international 'Shhh' signal (by placing my index finger vertically across my lips) or perhaps say something like, *"You can coach your players. You may not coach the umpires,"* and then get on with the game. If they ignore my instruction, they—at a minimum—get a green card.

[NFHS: A coach can be given a green card, a 5-minute yellow, or a red card. The team plays short for 5-minutes when a coach is yellow carded, one player per card (12.1.PENALTIES.1.b), and for the remained of the game if the coach is given a red card. The team does not play short when the coach only receives a green card (12.1.PENALTIES.a)]

[NCAA: There is no yellow card for college coaches. After a coach receives a green card, the only card left is red! Carding NCAA coaches never means that a player must leave the game or that a Penalty Stroke is to be taken.]

Even if I hadn't warned or carded the coach, if the coach tells me, *"You're a horrible umpire,"* I would red card the coach without hesitation. And, so should every umpire!

Here are some reasons that one would immediately use the red card. There are, of course, more reasons that call for an immediately use of a red card but this list should help.

- Coach makes negative physical <u>contact</u> with an umpire
- Coach threatens either umpire
- Coach is physically disruptive (throws a chair)
- Coach curses at either umpire or curses about either umpire
- Coach inspires severe misconduct in others

It is important to realize that EITHER umpire can card either coach even when and especially when the OTHER umpire is the target of the coach's misconduct. The umpire who is not under attack might be more relaxed and can certainly step up and card the coach.

 UMPIRES: Some coaches will make negative comments about the officiating that are sly/ indirect/ subversive. For example, you call a foul for a bad tackle and the coach says, "Nice tackle Iris." When this happens once, you really just have to bear with it but when it becomes a pattern, card the coach. I have been known to say, "No coach. It wasn't a nice tackle. If it had been, I wouldn't have had to blow the whistle."

MANAGING PLAYERS

The best ways for umpires to manage players is through understanding the game and what players are trying to do, judging play fairly, blowing the whistle decisively, showing primary signals with body language that helps the players get on with the game, correcting mistakes quickly. Umpires should say, *"I'm sorry. My fault,"* if they've pointed the wrong way. Then correct the direction and make sure BOTH teams have adapted before allowing play to restart. Being mindful of the little things early in the game (don't allow little pushes, don't allow encroachment on Free Hits and Side-Ins), and card players (and coaches) when they should be carded helps this game and the next.

 UMPIRES: Hunt for and call little pushes very early in the game. Make it clear that they won't be tolerated and use your cards for any subsequent offenses.

Umpires should use their whistle to communicate. They shouldn't verbalize their calls. They shouldn't call after players like this, *"Hey. Uh. You. Number, uh, 21. Blue player. With the red cleats. Stop that."*

Umpires who try to affect play with their voice often sound like an old nag. A few quick whistles (tweets) and a firm pointing of their finger to where they want the ball placed will get the umpire much further than, *"Red team. Bring the ball over here. No, not there. A little closer. HERE!"*

Umpire must always keep their promises. If an umpire tells the players to move the ball 'over here' and the players don't put the ball where the umpire indicated, the umpire must blow the whistle (stop the game) and MAKE THEM put the ball where it should be.

 UMPIRES: If you know the ball should be brought to point X, chances are so do most of the fans and certainly a large number of the players. If the athletes 'cheat' the starting point and you give up thinking, "Whatever," you just undermined yourself. If once you start positioning the Free Hit, make absolutely sure the players put it where YOU want it to go.

If the players are unsuccessful at getting the ball to where it need to be, i.e. if they get the positioning wrong again, the umpire should stop the clock, wait for the ball to get where it should be placed and consider carding the captain for delay of game before restarting the clock.

Talking with the Players

In the recent past there has been an emphasis on having umpires talk with the players rather than simply enforcing rules with the whistle. There are some hockey umpires who have taken the guidance to talk with the players to mean, sadly, never shut up! Speaking to the players a little should be supplementary to talking to the players with the whistle.

Umpires are well served by developing a collaborative relationship with the players so they can learn how the umpires are going to make calls in the grey fog where the rules are not perfectly clear. I strongly recommend that umpires develop a style of officiating that doesn't REQUIRE much talking. That said, umpires shouldn't hesitate to speak to the athletes if doing so will facilitate play or engender a collaborative relationship.

Remember, however, that umpires are barred from coaching and there is only so much talking one can do before they risk getting to coaching and an umpire who talks too much is likely to be way past annoying.

The conversations umpires want to have are one-on-one in nature, basically private conversations when it might help to say something like, *"Careful. Be careful."* If umpires know the players speak English, they can soften it up even more by saying, *"You've got to help make this game better. Please don't hack at the opponent's stick."*

Public Address Announcements: Unless the umpire is saying, *"Play on,"* when an umpire opens his or her mouth and speaks for more than one person to hear, it can be a bad thing— especially DURING play. Umpires should make sure they get a benefit if they speak. For example, one thing I end up saying during almost every game is, *"I'm never going to make you move the ball a little. I am only going to make you move at least 5 meters."*

I say that when a team is about to restart play from the wrong position and I've given my three quick whistles and, typically, give a big waving 'over there' motion with my arm. The player moves the ball about a yard and is about to restart play. I give three tweets again, say, *"Until we're at the circle I'm never going to make you move the ball a little bit, I am only going to make you move the ball a lot,"* and repeat my arm action. I do this because I don't want the players, fans, and coaches to think I'm being picky about ball placement. I'm announcing that, in fact, the last thing I'm doing is being picky so move the dang ball and move it a lot (over to within playing distance of the foul). The fans hear me say, *"I'm only going to move you at least 5 meters,"* and they start nodding in agreement.

I have gained a very important benefit with my little speech— the fans agree with me and it is unlikely that I'll have to repeat my speech to any other players.

MANAGING COACHES

Some of the most enthusiastic high school and college hockey coaches I have officiated games for were among the worst resources for rules information that govern the sport.

During the first period, the Blue team's coach was given a verbal warning, then a green card, and a yellow card. As is always the case, the umpires walked to the center of the competition surface to meet each other during the break.

One of the umpires who is clearly frustrated by the coach's behavior asks the other, *"How do you greet an umpire who has never read the rulebook?"* Without hesitating, the other umpire responds, *"Hello Coach."*

Coaching Knowledge

Some of us have been blessed by having the best coaches on the planet. They are students of hockey. They study other sports, soccer for example, just to see what they can take to make their hockey teams better. They read the rules, attend USA Field Hockey rules briefings, and even bought this book—all to improve their hockey knowledge. Hockey is in their blood.

Most have in their possession the latest copy of the rulebook but an incredibly high percentage admit (off the record) that they've never read it. Fewer have read a book like this that would give the coach insight into what to expect from the umpires. A surprising number don't attend pre-season briefings about rule changes. Most have never learned how to officiate. Worse, many coaches never even played hockey before getting their coaching job.

As evidence I present this story about what happened in a game I was officiating between two New Jersey colleges in the mid-1980's. During a break away, a defender intentionally fouled inside the circle by intentionally using the back of her stick. She deflected the ball over the back-line, preventing the ball from crossing in front of the goal where, naturally, attackers were waiting for a chance to score. I awarded a Penalty Stroke as the ball rolled down the hill that was behind the goal line. The coach of the defender started yelling (over and over again), *"How can it be a penalty stroke if the ball is still moving?"*

The coach demonstrated that she had only a very limited understanding of the rules. It was probably back when this coach was in ninth grade when she learned that if the goalkeeper sits on the ball a Penalty Stroke would be called. Of course, that isn't always true and, even when it is true, it is only ONE of many fouls that can cause a Penalty Stroke being called. (This is one of the chief reasons why I wrote this book.)

Awarding a Penalty Stroke to the attack rightly penalizes the defender in the example for an intentional foul inside the circle that had taken away a scoring opportunity from the attack. It always struck me odd that a coach of a COLLEGE team wouldn't know a rule so fundamental in the game but, she didn't and it wasn't the first or last time I was ever surprised by a coach for that sort of thing.

NOTE: *An additional problem that this situation presents the umpire is that, unfortunately, most parents and fans will not in a million years suspect that their child's college hockey coach doesn't know the rules that govern the sport of hockey. Instead they will immediately start thinking, "Yeah. How can that be a penalty stroke? The ball was still moving! Is that umpire blind or stupid?"*

A coach's behavior such as I've just described can make for an unpleasant environment (read that, can incite fans/can inspire misconduct in his or her players). This type of behavior by the coach has to be carded IMMEDIATELY.

Delay of Game (Coaches)

Encouraging a player to, *"Get up there,"* or *"Pass it,"* does not delay the game. It is certainly acceptable for a coach to yell out something along the lines of, *"Clementine! You're the left wing. Get outside of Celestine."*

Delay often happens on dead ball situations. The players are about to put the ball into play and all of a sudden a coach yells out an instruction that directly and immediately changes what the players were about to do. It might simply be that the coach shouts, *"Hit it to Emily."* That's fine. No delay (in fact, it might help move the play along). However, is a coach yells across the competition site to have a different player hit the ball into play,

"Quin! You take the hit," THAT can delay the game because time continues to run while Quin runs over to put the ball into play.

Changing the restarter isn't necessarily a big deal, especially when the coach is reminding a young players who should take the hit. Delay becomes a problem when either there is very little time left and the umpire judges that the coach was time wasting.

When a coach is 'over engineering' a situation, there is clear time wasting. *"No. No. No. Wait. Victoria, you switch with Bian. Kiet, you take the hit. No, I mean, Victoria, you go back and take the hit but I want you to hit it to Aaron so he can pass it to Barbara and then Barbara can hit it to Nick or Kiet."*

Possession should be given to the opponents.

Over-the-top instructions, moving the players around the competition surface like chess pieces, etc., are fine for a practice when the coach is preparing the team for game situations but, coaching during a competition that causes delay is not acceptable.

Recently I saw a team that had to stop prior to the taking of a Penalty Corner because the coach was delivering a relatively complex set of hand signals which told the team what Penalty Corner play the coach wanted executed. Coaching that causes athletes to stop and wait long enough that the flow of the game is 'broken' is causing a delay. An umpire might warn the coach one time, *"Coach. You're causing a delay of game on your team's Penalty Corners,"* because making that announcement reminds people within an earshot that 'delay of game' is not allowed AND, then, if the umpire does have to card, everyone will understand why it was the necessary action to take. It certainly doesn't make it look like the umpire is just 'making stuff up' as the game goes along.

Team Area versus Officiating Space

A crowded side-line is shown below.

An umpire has to be provided unobstructed space in order to run next to the game without having to watch where he/she is going.

Restrictions on coaches and other team personnel vary by

country and league/conference. The following reflects the restrictions common to play in the USA.

The coach is allowed to sit on his or her team bench, walk behind it, or otherwise stay at least 5 meters away from the side-line (see rule book for details). The coach, however, cannot move in a distracting manner. If a coach's movement distracts the umpire, the coach is violating this rule.

Coaches who stand/move within the umpire's officiating space (the area within 5 meters of the side-line) interfere with the umpire's field of vision and run the risk of injuring themselves or the umpire. Fear of injury or running into and potentially injuring the coach is a distraction. Card the coach!

Violations of the officiating space by a coach are not something that coaches need to be warned about—the rules are the warning—though an umpire might think to mention it during the pre-game meeting.

It is probably fair for the umpire to make one verbal warning that the fans can hear prior to carding the coach for leaving the coaching area. What the umpire might say is, *"Coach. You have to stay 5 meters back from the side-line so I can officiate from a proper position. I'm going to have to card you if you do not move back and stay back."*

Coaches who violate the boundary of the team area after a verbal reminder/caution are to be immediately carded.

 UMPIRES: Never give two verbal warnings for the same thing unless you enjoy being thought of as someone who makes empty threats. Keep your promises.

Unsportsmanlike Conduct (Coaches and Staff)

Umpires should immediately card the following types of coach and non-participating team personnel misconduct:

1. Making NEGATIVE PUBLIC COMMENTS about/toward/concerning the officiating (if someone beside the person who says it can hear it, it is public and if it's negative the coach must be carded IMMEDIATELY)

2. Proximity violations. A coach who enters the officiating space next to the side-line. When a coach comes within 4.5 meters/5 yards of the side-line consider giving the coach one verbal warning before carding the behavior. If the coach interferes with the umpire, they must be carded. If the coach is within the officiating space and there is a collision with the umpire, the coach must be red carded

3. Inciting negative reactions in others toward either umpire

NOTE: It is NOT true that only the head official (the one near the benches) can card the coaches and players on the bench. In fact, an accepted practice is for the more experienced umpire to offer the head official position to the less experienced umpire and to help manage the bench from the far side. The far-side umpire might also do well to award the card as a means of taking the "heat" off the head umpire. Further, it might be that the far-side umpire is simply more comfortable than a less experienced head official when it comes to carding a coach who is acting inappropriately.

MANAGING PARENTS AND FANS

Restrictions on fan behavior vary by country and league/conference and issues with fans tend to be handled by facility management. The following reflects the restrictions common to play in the USA.

Fans are great, even ones that don't understand the game very well. Rowdy fans are even better. Fans, however, are not allowed to cause problems. They may not threaten the umpires (but they can taunt the umpire a bit).

Fans are ONLY within the privilege they enjoy in attending a competition when they are watching the game and/or cheering FOR the athletes. When a fan elects to do other things, they are volunteering to give up the privilege to attend the event.

Fans may not curse at or make personal, derogatory, and/or sexual comments to any of the game's participants—the umpires, players, or coaches.

Umpires do NOT need to have thick skin to officiate. Umpires don't have to put up with verbal abuse (abusing an umpire goes beyond taunting an umpire). It is bad advice to tell umpires to be unaware (to not hear everything). An umpire's opinion about when a fan has stepped over a line is all that matters but here is some guidance:

Taunt: *"What game are you watching?"*

Taunt: *"Call it both ways!"*

Taunt: *"Let them play!"*

Taunt: *"You need a new pair of glasses!"*

Taunt: *"You're missing a good game!"*

Taunt: *"If you had another eye I'd call you Cyclops!"*

Taunt: *"I think you made a positioning error on that one."*

Personal: *"Let's go fatso!"*

Personal: *"You are an idiot!"*

Personal: *"You're pathetic!"*

Abusive: *"You're missing a good game! You're horrible! You're haven't got a clue. You...."*

NOTE: *All of these examples, if they were said by a coach, would be an immediate card in NFHS and NCAA games.*

Fans do not have the right or privilege to stand anywhere they want. For example, in a venue without adequate seating, fans may want to stand/sit relatively close to the sidelines but, they can't be within 10 meters of either side-line and the back-lines. Further, unless they are separated from the competition surface by a physical barrier, spectators are not allowed to be within 10 meters of any part of the back-line, including the goal-line.

While all of the things mentioned so far in this segment _can be_ dealt with by an umpire in NFHS games, they are actually the purview of the facility's management and are never an issue in a well-run facility. If an umpire doesn't know who is in charge of the site, the umpire works through the home team's head coach to address issues within the facility.

 UMPIRES: *In 2014, I saw an umpire at a college tournament stop the game and move people out from behind the back-line. The people were up a hill, at least 20 meters away, on the other side of a waist-high chain-link fence, and behind safety netting that rose 20 feet from the ground. With these actions, the umpire demonstrated a severe lack of understanding.*

UMPIRES: Although crowd control is a responsibility of the site manager, umpires are often left to control the sidelines and back-lines. If you have to, you should do so before a crowd has gathered. Doing so will avoid the subsequent need to move a larger number of people. Said another way, it is easier to move two people at the beginning of the game than waiting until halfway through the game when 50 people are sitting behind the back-lines in beach chairs.

IMPORTANT: Young children have been killed by shots that have gone wide of the goal. Do NOT let people watch from behind the back-lines near the goals. Watch out for children crossing behind the goals prior to Penalty Corners. If it happens, stop the clock, ask them to move (or have the home team coach take care of it) and then restart the clock.

REMOVING PLAYERS, COACHES, AND FANS

There will be times when a player's, coach's, and/or fan's behavior is such that the individual must be removed from the game and/or the facility.

<u>Player Removal</u>

When a player earns a yellow card, he or she is to sit out for at least 5 minutes and is allowed to return at the umpire's discretion (the umpire might say the suspension is for 7 minutes, 10 minutes, 14 minutes – any amount of time – or might extend a suspension if, for example, the player doesn't take a seat). NFHS rules say that the player is suspended for only 5 minutes or 10 minutes. Teams at all levels play with one less player during the time of the suspension for each green, yellow, and red carded player.

If the goalkeeper is suspended in an NFHS, a new goalkeeper must come into the game. A field player can replace the goalkeeper in NCAA and FIH games. As the carded goalkeeper must leave the game, The team's coach or captain will also identify a field player who will sit out so that the team is short one player for the suspended goalkeeper.

Suspended players should sit in a chair on the opposite side of the scorer's table from the suspended team's bench. Coaching a suspended player is NOT allowed.

When a player earns a red card, the player must leave the game and the team plays short for the remainder of the game, through and including any overtime/tiebreaker period.

[NFHS: A carded goalkeeper must leave the game and be replaced by another fully kitted goalkeeper (1.4.1). The coach identifies a field player to be removed at the start of the goalkeeper's suspension to ensure the team plays short. Suspended NFHS players/goalkeepers sit on their bench's side of the scorer's table. If the red card is flagrant in nature, some state athletic associations (members of the NFHS) apply additional penalties, including multiple game suspensions and inability for teams to play in postseason tournaments run by the state association in question.]

HOMEWORK: What do umpires do when the team is playing short at the end of regulation and the game goes into overtime? Is the team that would normally play overtime with seven athletes required to 'play short' with only six? Can a suspended player participate in a tiebreaker? Does it depend on whether the game is governed by the *Rules of Hockey* or the NFHS or NCAA modifications?

Coach Removal

In hockey games governed by the NFHS there are three things that must happen when a coach earns a red card:

1. The coach must immediately leave the facility/grounds

and their interactions with team personnel must cease (i.e., they can't go to the parking lot and communicate instructions by any means to any of the participants). If the red-carded coach does not adhere to these requirements, their team automatically forfeits the competition

2. A person employed by the school from which the coach was disqualified must be present to take charge of the team or the team automatically forfeits the competition

3. The opponent restarts play with the type of possession they already had or with a Free Hit if the red card was progressive or, if the NFHS coach was red carded for flagrant misconduct, play restarts with a Penalty Stroke (12.1.d.PENALTIES)

HOMEWORK (ask three different umpires): An umpire awards the Blue team in an NFHS game a Penalty Stroke and the coach from the Orange team curses at the umpire. The Blue team takes a Penalty Stroke due to the Orange coach's flagrant misconduct. The Blue team doesn't score. How is play restarted? With a Free Hit to the Orange team or with the Penalty Stroke that was awarded prior to the red card? If the Blue team scores on the Penalty Stroke awarded for the flagrant misconduct, how is play restarted? With the Orange team restarting play with a center-pass or with the Blue team taking the Penalty Stroke awarded prior to the red card? Okay. So, what if they do take two strokes and they score on the first one but miss the second. Now how is the game restarted?

The NFHS rulebook or state modification will detail other required actions that take place if the coach is red carded. For example, in the state of New Jersey, any NFHS team that earns three or more red cards, regardless of their nature (progressive or flagrant), cannot compete in the state tournament that New Jersey's high school athletic association runs.

Fan Removal

The question… *"What was that?"* … is probably said more at one high school hockey game in the USA than during all other life experiences combined. It seems as much a Pavlovian response to the sound of a whistle, conditioned by years of watching hockey next to other uninformed parents, as it is an honest quest for an answer.

Other fan favorites seem to include…

> *"Call one our way."*

> *"Get in the game."*

> *"You're missing a good game."*

> *"Ah! Call something!"* (Which is, typically, immediately followed by, *"Oh come on. Let the kids play."*)

As noted above, the only legitimate license that a fan enjoys at a game is watching the contest and the privilege of cheering for their team. If a fan becomes unruly, threatening, crude, obnoxious, etc., to any of the participants (either umpire, a specific player, a team, a coach, etc.), umpires can stop the game and have administrative personnel from the facility or the home team remove the fan from the competition site.

Obviously, it is helpful if the umpire is certain which fan it is that needs to be dealt with/removed BUT it is NOT necessary. Umpires can just direct site management, *"There is someone over there who must be removed."* Umpires, however, should not have any direct interaction with a disrespectful fan.

During a high school basketball game some fan(s) kept throwing little beads out onto the court. After several unsuccessful requests from the student announcer that the behavior stop, the less experienced umpire made an impromptu announcement stating that if another bead is thrown on to the court it would result in a technical foul against the home team.

The more experienced umpire grabbed the microphone away and said, *"I'm sorry but there has been a change of plans. If another bead is thrown, we will stop the game, send the teams into their locker rooms, clear the facility of fans, and then complete the game."*

There are many lessons to be learned from that true story. One, umpires should talk with each other before either one makes an announcement over a public address system. Two, safety of the players is a primary concern. Third, and this is most important, there is no rule requiring that there be any fans at a competition. In short, games don't have to be played with fans at the competition site, let alone unruly ones.

Here is what should happen when one or more NFHS fans become a problem and site management hasn't done its job and taken care of it before the umpires have to interrupt the game:

1. Stop game. Umpire stops game and goes to the home team coach and directs him or her to have the problem fan(s) immediately stop problematic behavior. The umpire should provide as much detail as possible but it might be something as simple as, *"A person over there (point) is complaining about every call I make and must stop. Take care of it right away."* Umpire restarts the game right away. Umpire doesn't wait to see whether the coach

actually does anything to complete the task. We want the interruption to be as short as possible.

2. [No change/issue returns.] Stop game (strike two). Umpire stops game and goes to the home team coach and directs him or her to cause the immediate removal of a fan(s) from the venue. Umpire tells the home team coach that the game will be restarted as soon as the umpire sees that the fan(s) are being addressed. Provide as much detail as possible about the fan(s) but it might be something as simple as, *"There are people over there who are making obscene comments about the players and must be removed."* Umpire waits to see that the fan is being addressed and then restarts the game.

3. [No change/issue returns.] Stop game (strike three). Go to the coaches of both teams and direct them to remove their players from the competition surface. Umpire tells the coaches that they will allow the game to be restarted as soon as all the fans are gone. Direct the home team coach to cause the fans to be removed. When all the fans are gone, allow the players and coaches to return and restart the game.

NOTE: Very often, hockey umpires are left dealing with the results of the uninformed teaching the 'rules' to the even less informed. In order to increase the knowledge and enjoyment of the modern game of hockey, area umpire associations should hold rule seminars before and/or during pre-season AND parents and fans should attend these sessions. Coaches should require their players to attend – at a minimum their team captains.

IMPORTANT: Players, coaches, parents, umpires, and fans should seek out rule training opportunities whenever possible. I publish an online rules and umpiring course. For course details, please visit the registration page at

UmpireHockey.com/enroll.

As much as we like to have them, fans are not required!

CHAPTER **6**

DO YOU KNOW ENOUGH TO UMPIRE

Here are the basic steps to becoming a certified hockey umpire.

Join Your National Association

Before you even finish reading this book and certainly before you do any officiating whatsoever, make sure that you have proper liability insurance coverage by joining your national association. In the USA that means joining USA Field Hockey. Of course, there are other membership benefits besides proper liability insurance but there are too many to list here. To join, visit the USA Field Hockey website (USAFieldHockey.com).

Take a Course

It is best to take an umpire training course offered by a

nationally certified Umpire Coach. In the USA, these trainers are certified by USA Field Hockey, the national governing body for the sport. I offer a course via the web that is suitable for beginners and experienced umpires. It covers field hockey and indoor hockey. You can take it at your convenience, from the comfort of your home computer, tablet, or smartphone. For detailed information and to enroll, please visit UmpireHockey.com.

Practice Officiating

There are typically summer camps available where umpires can begin to get practice. It is best to get an experienced umpire there to help you. Preferably this umpire would be a nationally certified Umpire Coach or an umpire who has (at least) recently attended a USA Field Hockey clinic for umpires or taken a refresher course by a nationally certified Umpire Coach within 24 months of the practice opportunity.

Even when practicing, never officiate alone. Here's what USA Field Hockey says about officiating without a partner:

"At no time should any hockey match, official or practice (outdoors or indoors, 11v11, 7v7, etc.), be officiated by only one umpire. It not only changes the dynamics for the umpires' decisions but greatly impacts the ability of the players and coaches to reach the standard of play they are trying to achieve."

That said, on a small field with 5 to 7 players per side, if there are no Penalty Corners to administer, using only one umpire is appropriate. Even the FIH condones this in their official rules for Hockey5s.

Beginners can practice officiating by watching other sports. Watch soccer and apply the *Rules of Hockey* to aerials (based on how soccer is played, hockey umpires would almost always blow their whistle if soccer was governed by the *Rules of Hockey*). Watch basketball and apply the *Rules of Hockey* while the center dribbles backwards into an opponent or the power forward sets a pick at the top of the key (hockey umpires would almost always blow their whistle if basketball were hockey because of obstruction and third-party obstruction).

Set Umpiring Goals

Do you only want to officiate games at the local middle school? How about games between varsity high school teams? How about the best high school or U19 club teams in your state? You might want to officiate at the college level. Do you want to officiate an NCAA championship? How about top men's clubs in the Euro Hockey League? What about the gold medal game at the Olympics?

The point of all those questions is to illustrate the many different levels of hockey available.

If you are an athlete with a recent playing connection to the modern game, why not set your sights on the Olympics?

You will find that not every officiating path leads to every level of officiating. Unfortunately, in the USA most umpire organizations only focus on middle school and high school level play. If your goal is to officiate college games, or even the Olympics, don't let yourself become trapped by a local association's limitations. A local association is not likely to be in a position to provide you the type of training and experience you'll need to reach your goals if they include umpiring at the college level and above.

The best way to advance to higher levels in the USA is to seek out opportunities with USA Field Hockey. You will likely want to join a local association anyway but, at least your eyes will be wide open and you'll know the limitations of the local association's ability to help you. Speaking of local associations…

Join a Local Umpire Association

To umpire on a regular basis, you'll probably need to join an umpire association that is relatively close to where you live. The quality of the services provided by local associations varies widely but, at a minimum, most will prove to be your only pipeline to local officiating opportunities. Chances are that the person who recommends this book or taught the course you took can put you in contact with the local umpire association. Still, always keep your eyes open to opportunities beyond the walls of your local association, especially if they're not progressive and you are.

Officiating at tournaments sponsored by USA Field Hockey is typically fun and very helpful (visit USAFieldHockey.com for more information about USA Field Hockey events).

Keep a Journal

Get yourself a journal. Or, perhaps there is a website for journaling. The online course at UmpireHockey.com provides a journaling environment. Record the date of EVERY umpiring outing along with notes. What was the weather like? Was the surface grass or turf, dry or wet? How do you feel you did? Was your partner kind or a jerk? What would you do better if you could do it over again? Doing this builds a resume of your games and a way to reflect on your experiences. If you don't do journal about your umpiring, there will come a time that you will regret not having done so.

Earn a Certification

There are four main parts to earning (and maintaining) your certification.

FIRST: Complete an umpire training program every four years
I hope your instructor makes this book required reading! ☺

SECOND: Take annual exam assessing your rules knowledge.

THIRD: Have your fitness tested, at a minimum, annually

FOURTH: Have formal evaluations of your on-field performances on a regular basis

The name of certification levels vary by country. USA Field Hockey currently offers the following:

STARTER UMPIRE: An umpire capable of officiating games between teams with athletes under 16 years of age, includes games between middle school and sub-varsity high school teams and U16 club teams

LEVEL I UMPIRE: An umpire capable of officiating games between teams with athletes under 19 years of age, includes games between varsity high school teams and U19 club teams

LEVEL II UMPIRE: An umpire capable of officiating games between teams with athletes under 21 years of age, a.k.a. games between college teams

LEVEL III UMPIRE: An umpire capable of officiating games between top level college teams and higher levels of play

In 2013 USA Field Hockey decided to publish my book called *JUMP IN! A Beginner's Guide To Umpiring Field Hockey*. Perhaps there will be a certification level someday for umpires who complete a training program named *Jump In*. An online copy is available online: http://issuu.com/crismaloney/docs/jump_in_

My newest book, *Field Hockey: The Beginner's Guide*, should prove helpful to fans, players, coaches, and future umpires because there are photographs of all of the umpiring signals with a simple rule explanation (http://www.FieldHockeyBook.com).

HOW DID __THAT__ UMPIRE GET __THIS__ GAME

As previously noted, membership in a local umpire association is typically required in order for an umpire to get games.

In every place that there are games, umpires are assigned to officiate them. If there is a person in the role, that person is usually called the assigner and they will either do the assigning the old fashioned way (by hand) or manage a web-based system.

A web-based system (I've used them all, as an umpire and assigner, and the one I prefer is ArbiterSports.com), allows either an assigner or the teams to manage their schedules and, through electronic communications, the umpires can receive invitations to accept level-appropriate assignments.

ArbiterSports.com also allows the assigner to set up a feature called "Self-Assign". This is great for umpires, assigners, and teams because if an umpire backs out of an assignment, another level-appropriate umpire can take the game without any additional work by the assigner or the teams.

The web-based systems are typically operated by the assigner or the local umpire association and paid for by membership fees charged to teams, umpires, and assigners. Assigners are typically hired by the teams (typically schools) for which the assigner is providing umpires.

For reasons lost to history, some assigners force umpires to pay a tax on their officiating earnings by charging the umpires a percentage of the money earned by the umpire at the games assigned. That makes no sense at all. There simply aren't enough umpires—anywhere—to justify the practice.

If the umpires just said, *"No,"* to this tax, the assigners would have no recourse. In fact, from a supply and demand perspective, the umpires might well tell the assigner, *"You pay me $5 and I'll take the game."*

You might say the practice of paying the assigner is like an agent earning a percentage of a movie actor's earnings—basically, the actors are paying a finder's fee to the agent for finding the actor work.

The difference is that there are far fewer movies made than there are actors. In fact, in 2004 there were 326 movies released (sorry, I forget the source) and there were 98,000 full time members of the Screen Actors Guild. That's 0.003 movies for every actor. With a ratio like that, I'd be happy to pay someone for finding me work too.

In hockey, the situation is just the reverse as the number of games far outnumbers the number of umpires. In my area alone, there are about 800 games that need to be officiated and, in a good year, about 40 umpires available to be assigned.

Under those types of conditions, it is simply illogical for an umpire to pay an assigner. The underlying 'supply and demand' dynamics are in favor of the people providing the supply (i.e. umpires). Assigners should look for more money from the organizations creating the demand (i.e. the schools and clubs with hockey teams).

Regardless of exactly how things operate in your area, the teams served by the officiating organization communicate the dates, times, and locations of their games, the officiating organization communicates the certification level of their umpires, and the umpires communicate their availability. If all the parties work in collaboration, the teams get to play and the umpires get to officiate.

Here are many of the variables that will impact the games to which umpires are assigned.

1. RANK: In any organization, there are umpires ranked at the top and, naturally, umpires ranked at the bottom. Obviously, one hopes these rankings are based on skill and not a good old girls/boys club. Only umpires with particularly high rankings should be assigned to late-round tournament games, games between rivals, and other priority games

2. FREQUENCY: An umpire should avoid officiating the same team two games in a row, or too many times in the same season, or in subsequent championship

appearances. An umpire doesn't want people asking, *"Isn't that the same umpire who was here last year?"* And, an umpire certainly won't want to officiate a game between a team they've never seen before and a team they've officiated in three recent games. Unfortunately, due to the ratio of umpires to games mentioned above, these ideals are often not possible to meet

3. BLOCKS: There will be many different reasons that an umpire has to be or will be 'blocked' from officiating certain games or teams

    ❖ DAYS OF THE WEEK: Maybe the umpire can only work on Tuesdays and Thursdays; maybe the umpire can only work weekends. The umpire blocks the days or the hours of the day that they cannot work

    ❖ DISTANCE: The distance an umpire can travel on any given day will restrict where the umpire can officiate. Perhaps on weekdays the umpire has to be within 10 miles of their house but on weekends they can drive 100 miles

    ❖ TEAMS/COACHES/UMPIRES: You can't please all the people all the time and, for any number of reasons, any given umpire may be 'blocked' by a team, a coach, an athletic director, or another umpire. An umpire may not be blocked at all. Or, only be blocked from doing a certain team's home games until a certain group of athletes graduate (and so do their parents, if you know what I mean) or a team might say,

"We never want to see that umpire again!" An umpire might not want to work with one of the umpires in the local organization each joined. Some organizations don't allow teams to block an umpire for regular season games but do allow blocks during tournaments. Some organizations don't let umpires block other umpires. Most organizations will limit the length of time an umpire can be blocked when the block is for personal reasons

❖ SPHERE OF INFLUENCE/CONFLICTS OF INTEREST: An umpire might be blocked if they are connected in some way to a team. For example, if an umpire were the head coach of Team A last year and they have a history of beating Team B in championship games but the team always lost to Team C, that umpire will be blocked from officiating any game involving Team A and even games between Team B and Team C (because, should Team B win, the outcome of the game might be clouded by an accusation that the umpire/former coach helped Team B beat Team C so the old team would eventually win the championship). In a less complicated example, that umpire might be blocked from officiating in the former team's division/league for a certain period of time (perhaps 4 years). Young umpires might block a team because they just played for them last year. Maybe the umpire has never even played hockey but they're a student at the school in question.

Or, maybe the umpire can't do any 'Main Street High School' games because they have a child or sibling that is a student there or the umpire's spouse is the principal

❖ FAMILIARITY: As implied above, if it is reasonable, an umpire should block teams that they've seen too often

Umpires should go overboard to ensure that there isn't even an appearance of a conflict of interest. That means that umpires shouldn't accept an assignment if they should have been blocked in the first place. If the umpire is assigned to a game that they know they shouldn't work, they can't claim it wasn't their fault because, *"The assigner made me do it."* Sorry. That's a bucket that doesn't hold water. The umpire knows best where they should not work.

Conflicts aren't always about an ability to be impartial. One time I was called and asked to officiate a game that had to be turned back at the last minute by an umpire who wasn't feeling well. I made it clear to the assigner that my close family relative was a teacher at one of the schools involved. The assigner asked me if that would impact my ability to be impartial. I said, *"No."* I took the assignment and I officiated impartially. I wasn't unfair to the other team by being too lenient on the school for which my relative taught and I wasn't unfair to the team from my relative's workplace by being too hard on them. I was just fair.

Unfortunately, however, one of the girls on the team from my relative's school came up behind an opponent, threw down her stick and tried to push the opponent to the ground (payback for something that had happened earlier). The girl's actions earned her a red card (from me) and because of the flagrant nature of the foul, the player was not only out for the rest of that game, she also was barred from playing in the next two games (a special penalty created by the state athletic association).

To make matters worse for the team, the athlete who earned the red card was the team's star player and the team was on the edge of making, for the first time, a major tournament.

While I had no problem with the situation, my relative said she spent the next few weeks hearing how I gave their star player a red card and now they might not go to the big tournament.

Imagine if instead one of my children was a student at the school and these comments were directed at a child.

The moral of the story? Just because the umpire can be impartial doesn't mean that the umpire should accept every assignment they're offered.

 UMPIRES: Remember, the assigner's priorities are not necessarily aligned with an umpire's. The assigner's job is to get games covered.

IMPORTANT: Umpires should absolutely not accept assignments to work at schools with which they have an "in-building" connection.

TURNING BACK GAMES

As the story above points out, every so often something comes up and the umpire isn't able to officiate a game they've previously accepted. While different organizations, systems, and assigners handle this situation differently, all umpires should *IMMEDIATELY* follow whatever the prescribed procedures are when they have to 'turn back' a game they have accepted to officiate.

CHAPTER 8

UMPIRES ON GAME DAY

The umpires have to wear shirts that are different from those of the competing teams. Most officiating organizations will have a couple of 'approved' shirts from which to pick. USA Field Hockey used to sell a set of shirts (three different colors) on their website but has, at least unofficially, switched to a single color shirt for umpires at their events.

Over the course of the last few years, many umpire associations have been settling on one or two near-fluorescent colored shirts and, so far, no teams are wearing similarly colored uniforms.

 UMPIRES: Never wear zebra stripes. In hockey, umpires have to look for each other frequently and zebra stripes are 'designed' to serve as camouflage—helping to

make relatively large animals difficult for very successful predators, like lions, to see when they're running around outside.

Weather

Umpires should be well aware of what the weather is going to be like. There aren't many thunderstorms in September, October, and November but umpires should know if the area is expecting lightning. If it will be raining, I would advise that umpires avoid wearing rain gear—you want to look like you're officiating, no one said that means umpires have to be dry. The athletes aren't wearing rain gear; umpires are part of the game, not spectators. Even if it is really cold, I would avoid bundling up any more than the athletes. Wear gloves but not a parka! Wear something to cover the ears (if you must) but not a hood!

IMPORTANT: Know the procedures for lightning (available from your local organization).

Going to the Game

If at all possible, umpiring partners should arrive at the same time. In fact, it's even better to arrange to meet a few miles from the site—a diner, the mall, local grocery store—and arrive in the same car.

 UMPIRES: Never park in a spot marked for umpires or officials. Think about it.

Arrival

If the umpires weren't able to drive together, neither umpire should go to the competition surface before the other umpire arrives. Umpires or umpire associations can set up a 'safety time' and if the other umpire hasn't shown up by 'then' the umpire who is already on site can go to the competition surface alone.

At the site of a competition, an umpire should ONLY want to be seen shoulder to shoulder with their officiating partner. As soon as anyone can see either umpire, the umpire should look like they are part of a team.

Once together, the umpires should say hello to the coaches and any players with whom they cross paths.

Except to say, *"Hello,"* and perhaps a quick handshake upon arrival (never a hug), one umpire shouldn't appear to be meeting with one coach or one captain. Further, neither umpire nor the team of umpires should have extended conversations with only one coach. It doesn't look fair. If the umpires have to have an extended conversation with only one coach, they must go to the other team's coach to speak with that coach about the conversation for what would appear to be about the same amount of time. The fact of the matter is that umpires are there to officiate, and there is little reason to have extended conversations with the coaches.

[NFHS: By rule (2.2.1.f), umpires can review the scorebook at the end of each quarter. Years ago, umpires officiating NFHS games were asked to sign the scorebook at the end of the game to, essentially, authenticate the score and sign out. Now, umpires of NFHS high school games typically sign in.]

 UMPIRES: *When signing the rule book, also print your name.*

Warming up

Umpires are (should be) athletes too. Before each game, all athletes need to warm up.

UMPIRES: Here's a suggested warm up. Jog around the competition surface about four times with your officiating partner. If your partner tells you that they don't warm up, jog without them. Don't be lazy. You're an athlete, prepare like one. Each time you run around the competition site, take a smaller and smaller route BUT go behind the goals each time. On your final lap, stop at each goal—make sure the goal is set properly behind the goal-line, the netting is firmly attached and in good repair, everywhere. You don't want the ball to go flying through the netting! Make sure the netting attaches to the posts and crossbar, and make sure that the 18 inch goal boards are attached properly. Travel at least once outside the back-lines and sidelines of the competition surface. This is all part of the officiating space and you have to make sure it is safe (for you and the athletes). Look for dangerous environmental situations (holes, ditches, muddy spots, hoses, broken glass, etc.).

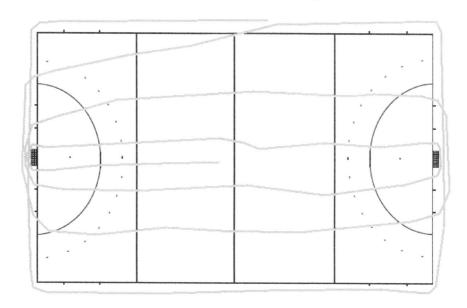

IMPORTANT: Check for ALL markings. Nothing like getting into the game and being surprised there is no mark for Penalty Corner insertions, etc. Do the markings look right? Is the Penalty Stroke mark where it should be? On competition surfaces lined for multiple sports, do you know which color is for hockey? Do the line colors change (white sidelines with blue back-lines). Do you and your partner agree that 'that' is the stroke mark?

By the way, the 'warming-up' part of this is only one aspect of the jog. What you're doing also helps visually establish the umpires as a team—to the players, coaches, parents, fans—and it gives you and your partner additional time to discuss how you will work together especially as you actually cross over areas of the competition surface you want to discuss.

As just mentioned, an important part of your 'warm up' is to make sure you and your partner are on the same page—or at the very least understand how you are going to be officiating differently. While it is better to be working the same way, it is critical to know what to expect. Having said that, if the other umpire says something crazy like, *"And I'm going to call in your circle,"* you have to tell him or her that such a practice is simply not acceptable.

 UMPIRES: *If someone were to call in your circle, call time-out, discuss the situation with your partner, and restart play with a Bully.*

If you're umpiring and your partner says, *"Don't give me big signals when I look for help with calls in my circle,"* say in response, *"I will be ready to give you assistance whenever you look to me. Whenever I look for help I find there are so many people running back and forth in front of me that I want my partner to show me the biggest signal they can and, I'm*

afraid, I like that so much that I've developed the same habit."

Which Umpire Should Be Table Side

In umpiring parlance there are two sides of the competition surface—table side and far side. Many umpires think that being table side is the 'harder' side because that's the side with coaches. Fair enough but, more often than not, the far side is typically the side with the fans. There are also umpires who feel that being the table side umpire is more prestigious. Regardless, it is important that all umpires get experience on both sides of the competition surface.

There are many ways to determine which umpire will be taking the position on the table side of the competition site. Perhaps one of the umpires was just at this particular site and was table side or far side. They should say so and offer to take the other side. Maybe there is reason to be on one side or the other, perhaps the sun will be in one of the umpire's eyes and only one of the umpires has a brim to shield his or her eyes from the sun. Perhaps, one of the umpires recently had a bad experience with one of the coaches, which can mean it is better to be table side again. If all things are otherwise equal, the more senior umpire will typically ask the other umpire, *"Which side do you want today?"*

If both umpires want/don't want table side, flip a coin.

Pre-Game

Just like the pilot of an aircraft, there are certain 'pre-flight' checks that umpires must go through before the start of the game (before take-off) to help make sure they don't crash once the game gets started. Some of those things have already been described. Still, there is more to do.

WATCH THE PLAYERS WARMING UP

Umpires learn a lot about what they'll see during the upcoming game by watching the athletes practice their individual and team skills. Are any of the athletes using small aerial dodges (what I call, "close-control, three-dimensional play")? Are any of the athletes practicing high flicks traveling long distances down the competition surface? What kind of Penalty Corners are they practicing? Is anyone practicing illegal skills (like hitting hard with an edge on the forehand side)?

At the 2008 National Futures Championship in Virginia Beach, Virginia, I was watching the teams and umpires prior to the start of one of the games. The umpires weren't watching the players warm up. Within about two minutes I noticed that one of the athletes, basically right under the noses of the umpires, was hitting the ball back and forth with her teammates using the forehand edge action that the FIH, with a good deal of emphasis, ruled as an illegal skill in 2006.

Not surprisingly, during the game the athlete used the illegal skill for a hard hit that traveled from one 35-yard line, across the center-line, to the other 35-yard line. Neither umpire noticed that the athlete used an illegal action—both should have. The FIH wants this action eliminated from the game.

Sooner or later you'll hear the phrase, preventative umpiring. This would have been a great time to use it. Had I been officiating the game and saw the athlete using the illegal skill during her warm ups, I would have said to the athlete practicing this illegal skill, *"You're not going to hit like that during the game, are you?"* And, then I would have made sure she understood that what she was practicing was illegal. It would have taken all of 15 seconds and the game would not have included the illegal skill.

CHECKING THE GOALS

An umpire's primary concerns with the goal are to:

- Ensure that there are no openings in the netting or goal boards through which a shot can escape

- Check that the goals are positioned properly just behind the goal-lines

- Check that the competition surface sides of the posts and crossbars that face the competition surface are flat

MEETING WITH THE TIMEKEEPER & SCOREKEEPER

A good time for umpires to meet with the timekeeper and scorekeeper (timer and scorer) is after the umpires complete their warm up.

During lower level games, the timer and scorer are typically young people who spend much of their time chitchatting about things that have nothing to do with the game at hand. Regardless of their age, umpires should establish a relationship of trust with the timekeeper and the scorekeeper and make sure they understand their responsibilities.

There are three really important questions umpires should ask a timekeeper:

- *"Can you show me the signal we give when we want you to stop the clock?"*

- *"How will you confirm to me that you've seen my signal and stopped the clock?" (This only matters if there is no visible clock.)*

- *You know that you MUST allow the clock on the scoreboard run to zero, right?*

If the competition site has a scoreboard clock or other visible clock that can be seen by the participants and fans, it is by rule the official clock and must, also by rule, count all the way down to zero—even if it means that a horn will sound during a Penalty Corner.

The umpires should have the scorekeeper show them where he or she will record goals and cards in the scorebook.

Ask the scorekeeper:

- *"Will you be sure to get the names and numbers of all the players in the book?"*

- *"Can you show me where the field players make their substitutions? What about the goalkeepers?"*

Basically, umpires want to make sure that the scorekeeper and timekeeper know their responsibilities and that the umpires are expecting help from them during the game.

If the umpires demonstrate that they're going to take the scorekeeper and timekeeper seriously, the scorekeeper and timekeeper will take their responsibilities seriously. This pre-game conversation will also give the umpires insight into how much handholding they might have to do during the competition and also helps younger timekeepers and scorekeepers understand the importance of their roles.

 UMPIRES: At the end of the game, thank the timekeeper and scorekeeper for their help. Tell them, "You did a good job. You should become an umpire!"

CHECKING THE GAME BALLS

There usually isn't a problem with game balls BUT no manufacturing process is perfect and sometimes a ball is made that is out-of-balance at its core. You can see a hockey ball with this problem when it starts 'behaving badly' as it rolls across synthetic/turf competition surfaces. When passed, the ball can be seen rapidly 'vibrating' as it travels to its destination. Luckily, it is very easy to find out if a hockey ball has this problem BEFORE the competition begins.

If the center of gravity of a hockey ball is off center it will wobble when it's tossed into the air in a manner that rotates the ball on its axis. To see if the center of gravity of any of the hockey balls you're about to play with are off center all you need to do is toss each hockey ball into the air (twice).

The first time, toss the ball so that the logo rotates around the ball. The second time you toss the ball, toss it in such a way that the logo spins in one position on the side of the ball. You must do both tosses to complete the test. If the core is off-center, you will see the ball wobble as it spins overhead in the air on one of the tosses.

Each time, toss the ball into the air in such a way that the ball is spinning very quickly and goes high enough that you have time to watch the ball as it spins above your head.

NOTE: If you're a horrible catch, be careful as the ball will return to Earth!

CHECKING PLAYER EQUIPMENT

During the time that the teams are warming up, umpires should have a look at the players and their equipment. Unless a formal stick check is planned, this is when the umpires should perform stick checks; see if the athletes have proper numbers on their shirts; is everyone wearing shin guards; see who is wearing the captain's band, etc.

In some areas, teams are asked to line up prior to the game so the athletes and sticks can be checked as part of a more formal process. Each team lines up on the side-line in front of their team's bench. All the players should bring every stick they brought to the competition site, not just the ones they plan to use during the game. The sticks should be held near the toe; toe end up so the umpires can quickly check to make sure that the end of the stick is not splintering. Umpires can also check for excessive taping and make sure any stick with lots of tape can still fit through the stick ring. Of course, umpires are free to check any or all sticks regardless of whether they've been taped.

Umpires should check all the sticks to be used by goalkeepers regardless of whether they have any tape on them.

 UMPIRES: Don't disqualify a keeper's stick for failing to pass through your ring if it fails because the outside diameter of your stick ring is too big to make tight turns.

If a stick has to be disqualified, it is taken from the athlete and left at the scorer's table. It must remain there until the game has ended or until the stick has been fixed.

Obviously, if the umpire sees something that he or she thinks is dangerous, the athlete has to remove it. In 30 years of officiating, I've only had one person remove jewelry that I felt was dangerous. It was during an indoor match and I had to ask a woman to take off her engagement ring because the diamond was HUGE and, seriously, it looked like she could stab someone with it!

I coached a girl who had a tiny ear piercing over the antitragus that would probably require surgery to remove. Would it really be 'practical' for an umpire to have insisted that the piercing be removed?

NOTE: Really, really thorough player and equipment checks can be a good ~~*stalling tactic*~~ *use of time if your partner has not arrived on time.*

[NFHS (1.9.1.b): The head coaches are responsible for certifying that all the athletes are legally equipped. Umpires sometimes have to verify the veracity of the head coach's claim that his/her athletes are using legal equipment (for example, checking to see if sticks actually fit through a metal ring to verify sticks do not exceed the legal width of 51mm). Once the game begins, if an NFHS player is found to be illegally equipped, the offending player is carded (8.2.i-j.]

MEETING OF UMPIRES, CAPTAINS, AND COACHES

Before the game is to begin the umpires hold an official meeting with the captains. The main purpose of this meeting is to flip a coin to determine how the game will begin. In NFHS games, the meeting is held with the captains and the head coaches (though the coaches are not required to stay for the whole meeting).

Should this pre-game meeting be held in an organized or haphazard way? Is there a plan? Where on the competition surface should the meeting take place? Where should everyone stand? How should the umpires be dressed?

NOTE: Although there are important administrative tasks that must be completed, we would be well served is everyone approaches the meeting with an understanding that the overarching goal of the meeting is to get to the coin toss as quickly as possible so we can start playing hockey! The meeting should take less than 90 seconds and never more than two minutes.

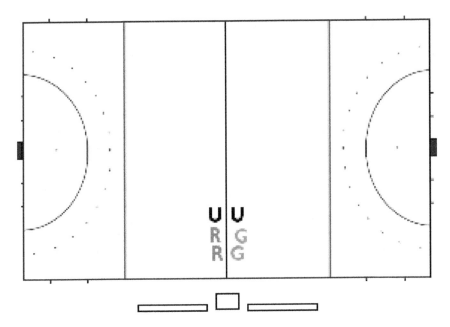

The meeting should take place as far in advance of "game time" as possible – as soon as the umpires and teams are there, get it done! This allows the players and coaches to focus on final preparations as game time approaches. There is no reason to wait and hold the meeting just before the game begins unless the coin toss is to be part of a broadcast.

When the umpires are meeting with the captains before the competition begins, the umpires should be dressed in the uniform they will be wearing while they're officiating. The umpires should not be wearing hoodies, parkas, etc., or any other clothing that they won't be wearing during the game.

The umpires should stand next to each other, shoulder to shoulder, on either side of the center-line, and near the table-side sideline. There is no rule dictating that the meeting take place halfway between the sidelines. Traditionally, the teams will participate in the meeting on opposite sides of the center-line, on the side closest to their team area. This positioning, however, does not have to be over orchestrated.

In the old days hockey umpires would stand apart from each other, on opposite ends of the meeting space – as if they're opponents. This is incorrect for two reasons. First, it separates the umpiring team. Until separated by the necessity of being on opposite sidelines, the umpires should always be together, standing shoulder to shoulder. Second, the captains are made to look back and forth like they're watching a tennis match as the umpires speak. Generally, this incorrect positioning is taken by 'old timers' without recent training.

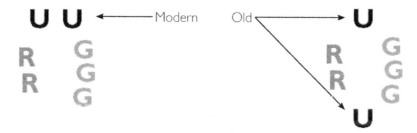

MEETING PROCEDURES ("**NIC**")

In their meeting with the captains, the umpiring team should focus on stepping through the NIC process (Names, Inspection, and Coin) and getting the game started with as little pomp and circumstance as possible. I suggest that the table-side umpire ask for the names of the captains and that the other umpire gives the inspection report. The coin toss can then be done by the table-side umpire. Umpires should confirm this division of responsibility prior to the start of the meeting.

N = **Names**: The umpires should make sure they have the *name* of each team's captain. Most times in the USA, teams will send multiple captains to the meeting. The umpires need to identify the 'speaking captain' (said another way, the 'real' captain).

The name and number of each speaking captain should be written down on each umpire's recording material.

 UMPIRES: Make a point of using each captain's name during the meeting. This helps establish rapport between the umpires and the captains – improving sportsmanship.

NOTE: Some states associations are having umpires read a sportsmanship announcement before games. This is to be read BY THE UMPIRES and NOT given to the athletes to read.

[NFHS (2.1.4.c): The umpires must meet with the head coaches and captains from both teams for the coaches' verification that the players are properly equipped and the coin toss. Each head coach must certify that all players' uniforms and equipment are legal. I recommend that umpires do this at the very beginning of the meeting so the coaches can leave if they are so inclined. The rest of the time can be used for the umpires and captains to meet. The meeting should not take more than 90 seconds. Even where state associations require the reading of a sportsmanship announcement, these meetings should only rarely extend beyond 90 seconds.]

One of the most important things the umpires can say to the captains is, *"Remember, you are responsible for the actions of your teammates, whether they're in the game or on the bench."*

[NFHS/NCAA: In NFHS and NCAA games, the captains are responsible only for the players on the field. The head coach is responsible for substitutes and non-participating team personnel on the bench and in the team area.]

I = Inspection: The second most important thing the umpires should do is go over what the umpires learned as they inspected the playing area. On multipurpose fields, this means reporting to the captains what color lines will be used during the game (blue sidelines, yellow circles, black goal-lines, etc.).

Other inspection items might include mentioning where the surface is mismarked, what to do if a ball rolls under the fence/into the pond, and other things specific to the venue. Discuss any special circumstances that might impact the game—the possibility of an approaching storm, a visible clock with a horn that cannot be disabled, whether tie will be broken, etc.

Early in the season or in a tournament, umpires might also go over how they expect the captain to work with the umpires. For example, what the umpires expect the captains to do if there is a BIG whistle or worse, a carding.

 UMPIRES: Here's an example of what might be said. "Niki. Melissa. If you hear me use a long, loud whistle after a foul, that's also your signal to talk with your player and make sure they know that they should never do whatever that whistle was for again. If I'm carding one of your teammates and you want to come over to be with them, that's up to you. The important thing is to understand that I expect you to help ensure we have a great game here today. I will work with you. You work with me. If something happens that you think we really got wrong—perhaps you think a player kicked the ball into the goal—go to the umpire in that circle and ask us to check with each other. By the way, make sure your coaches understand that if they have a question, they should ask you to bring it to the umpires."

C = **Coin**: Finally, the coin toss to determine how the match will begin. In short, which team will defend which goal and which team will begin the game in possession of the ball. The visiting team calls the coin in the air and the umpire should allow the coin to land on the ground.

Generally speaking, the visiting team is calling heads or tails. If a specialty coin is being used, such as the UmpireHockey.com coin, the umpire must make sure, *before the toss*, that the captains from both teams know either which side represent heads or to call the relevant information (it might be a color, such as "red", or a specific image, such as "whistle").

It is accepted practice, particularly at the beginning of a tournament or playing season, to make sure the captains are aware of any brand new rules or interpretations that would help the game but, as I said, this meeting is not to be a rules briefing.

Captains are responsible for bringing up anything out of the ordinary that they should share about today's game. I was told by one captain that midway through the game there would be a presentation of flowers to seniors. Another captain wanted me to know that one of her teammates was deaf and couldn't hear the whistle. Many captains will ask a question about the rules based on something that happened in their last game. Umpires can't give rule seminars just before game time but can try to answer a captain's question quickly and succinctly. If the captain doesn't understand your answer or wants more and more information, you have to say something like, *"I'm sorry but now really isn't the time to go into this much detail about the rules. We've got to play the game now."*

<u>Tips for Umpires from the World of Public Speaking</u>

If a captain does have a question, repeat it to the captain who didn't ask it. Then, ask the captain who asked the question if you've got the question right. When you get agreement on what the question was from the captain, begin by answering it toward the other team's captain. At the end of answering the question, be sure to return to the captain who asked the question and confirm, *"Does that answer your question?"* When they confirm, you say, *"Okay. If there aren't any more questions, let's do the coin toss."*

Sometimes, however, you don't want to get confirmation. You might get a question like this. *"How are you going to call danger because last week the umpire never called danger so we were wondering how you would call danger...and also what about obstruction?"*

What you don't want to do is start demonstrating the jumping jack space!

What I recommend saying is something like, *"That kind of call is very important to both of us. We make those judgment calls based on how we've been trained. Every game and each situation is unique but we'll both do our best. If there aren't any more questions, let's do the coin toss."*

First Whistle

The 'table side umpire' will blow the first whistle to start the game. Immediately prior to starting the game that umpire:

- Checks to see if the goalkeepers appear to be ready (they've got the longest distance to go)

- Confirms that the timer is ready to start the clock

- Makes sure that the other umpire is ready

- Optionally asks the captain of each team if their teams are ready (use names if you do)

There is a habit (a bad habit) in the USA of asking the goalkeepers if they are ready. We hear it before so many hockey games, *"Goalkeepers are you ready?"* Really? Are umpires SO BLIND that they can't see if the giant goalkeepers are ready?

 UMPIRES: Don't fall victim to this 'goalkeepers are you ready' foolishness. You've just spent time in your meeting with the captains emphasizing how you're going to be working with them and describing how you want them to work with you so don't, at your first opportunity, cut them out of the picture. If you're not sure if a goalkeeper or any other player is ready, ask the captain! "Brooke. Keely. Are your teams ready?"

When each of the criteria is met, the umpires puts his or her whistle to their mouth, turns their attention to the center pass, and blows their whistle long and loud to start the game.

Post-Goal

After a goal, before signaling the restart of play, both umpires are required to record the event on their recording materials. In NFHS games, the table-side umpire makes sure that the scorekeeper records the goal.

As mentioned above, the umpire who will blow the whistle to restart play after a goal must check with his or her partner before restarting play! Though necessary, it is very embarrassing for an umpire to have to whistle to re-set the restart because he or she wasn't ready when the other umpire blindly blew his or her whistle.

 UMPIRES: If the other umpire ever restarts play before you're ready, quickly blow your whistle three times to stop play. Have the players reset while you finish whatever it was you were doing. Do NOT stop what you were doing! You don't have to have a conversation about it. Clearly, you're only doing something that's important, like recording the score. Finish. Then point to your partner in such a way that they know they can start the game again.

There are some areas in America where the player who scores is told to go retrieve the ball and carry it up to the center-line. This is not supported by the rules and I have only ever seen this done by girls playing high school hockey. It is absolutely inappropriate for umpires to tell players who score to carry the ball up to the center-line.

Post-Game

When the game ends, and before either umpire goes to the side-line, they first greet each other in the center of the competition surface, check to see that their recordings of game events (goals, cards, time-outs) are in agreement, and then walk together to the officials table to gather their belongings and leave the competition site together. Umpires should NOT get the hockey ball.

 UMPIRES: Walk with each other to your transportation. It can be advisable to become 'non-umpires' by putting on a jacket over your uniform. Walk off the competition surface side by side, shoulder to shoulder, even if you're really angry with your partner for some reason. (It'll happen. Get over it.)

Coaches Evaluating Umpires

Umpires are never asked to evaluate coaches after umpiring a game. What would that even look like? *"Please rate the coach's penalty corner plays on a scale from 1 to 5."*

Yet, on more than one occasion, umpire associations have written to me seeking advice because they were planning on making a feedback form for coaches to use to evaluate each umpire after every game.

It has typically been difficult for me to respond because there is usually no reason given as to why these evaluation forms are being developed. What I often learn is that there isn't an underlying problem that having the form is trying to address. Rather, it's just that the umpire association thought it would be a "nice idea" to ask coaches for feedback—just something the association ought to do.

Although always well intentioned, asking coaches to provide feedback on all the officials calling a game demonstrates a severe lack of respect for the coaching community.

Coaches have a responsibility to watch their athletes perform during games. The coach's job is to make game day changes and modify upcoming practice sessions in preparation for the team's next competition based on the coach's close attention to the performance of the players.

It's beyond presumptuous to think that a coach is in a position to offer valuable feedback on multiple officials if at the same time they're watching their athletes throughout the course of a game.

All that said, certified umpire evaluators can't possibly be at every game so it is very tempting to ask coaches to do some work for the umpire association.

The question becomes, despite the built-in weaknesses, is it possible to construct a plan for getting feedback from people who aren't trained to umpire, let alone to evaluate umpires, that can help the umpire association?

The first thing umpire associations interested in developing a feedback plan have to do is realize that coaches are not the only resource present at every game—team captains are an additional resource. If an association is going to collect feedback from coaches, it should also collect feedback from the team captains, even at the high school level. Think about it. Umpires are at the game for the players. It would never make sense to collect feedback about the umpires and NOT ask the players.

SERIOUS UNDERTAKING

No one likes to have their time wasted so it would be best if the association can go beyond explaining the features of the program and also describe how taking the time to provide feedback will benefit the local coaches and players.

Therefore, one of the first things an umpire association should do before going down this path is to decide how the information it collects will help the association raise the standard of umpiring that the association's umpires are providing. In this part of the process the umpire association must create very specific, objective and measurable goals for using the feedback that's collected.

The association should also know how it will and won't use the data collected on feedback forms. Planning for how the data will be turned into actionable information is critical. For example, the association would want to take immediate individual corrective training if it learned that pre-game meetings with captains and coaches were taking longer than necessary. At the same time, it would never want to use the information to determine a preference list of a coach's favorite umpires. You don't have to be a rocket scientist to know what a dangerous idea that is.

Questions the umpire association needs to answer are:

1. Can the answers to the feedback questions be aggregated so the association can see trends and so umpires can compare himself/herself to the association as a whole?
2. Will individual feedback forms be shared with any of the evaluated umpires or will only aggregated data be shared?
3. Who will do the aggregation/who will have access to the feedback forms?
4. When will feedback be shared/tabulated—every time feedback is received, only after at least X number of evaluations are received, at a mid-season and/or end of the season meeting, just prior to the start of the next season?
5. Will feedback from all submitted forms be considered or will the forms only be considered when the coaches and captains from both teams (i.e. the winning and losing teams) submit their forms?
6. How will the feedback forms be distributed and collected? Will this all take place online or will the feedback forms be printed? How will printed forms be distributed and when – before the season, before each game, after each game, by who, to who?
7. Is the program worth launching if it isn't required by the athletic directors (the coaches bosses)?
8. When/how will the program be evaluated to determine whether the program should be continued? What metrics will be used to assess the program? For example, should an umpire association continue this type of evaluation program if only 70% of the coaches complete an evaluation of both umpires on 70% of their games?

All of those questions and more have to be established before the association can determine the questions that will be asked on the feedback form.

Certainly, anything an association asks coaches and captains to observe would have to focus on those things that can be observed when the game is not being contested—during the game the coaches and players aren't focused on the umpires. It might be reasonable, however, to collect feedback concerning the conduct displayed by the umpires before the game begins, during breaks, and after the game.

Coaches and team captains can observe, without distraction from their core responsibilities, the following:

1. Did the umpires show up on time?
2. Did the umpires arrive to the field together, as a pair?
3. Did the umpires come to the meeting with the captains and head coaches in their uniform—shirt tucked in, jackets off, etc.? In short, did the umpires look like they were there to do a job or did they look like spectators?
4. Did the umpires complete the meeting with the captains and head coaches in less than 90 seconds?
5. Did the umpires show primary signals first and long enough for the player to know which direction play was awarded or did they stall the game by showing secondary signals first?
6. Did the umpires record game events (goals and cards)?
7. When carding, did the umpire show the card, direct the player off the field, and immediately restart play or did the umpire stall the game by [a] having a conversation with the athlete or [b] waiting for the athlete to leave the field before allowing play to resume?
8. Did the umpires meet together in the center of the field at during breaks and at the end of the game before moving off the field?
9. Did either umpire make calls in the circle on their left?

That's a long list and maybe you can think of other questions. I would pick three things that the association would like to see improved upon during the season.

The one thing an umpire association absolutely must NOT do is suggest that the coaches have the training (and time) to assess subjective areas of two umpires' performances—decision making, seeing fouls, judgment, which card to apply, etc. Further, the questions must not waiver from those things for which the umpires are actually accountable.

One really bad feedback question a field hockey association was considering was, "Did the umpires communicate well with the coaches?" That question is bad for two reasons.

First, it suggests that umpires are required to communicate with coaches, and do it well. Field hockey umpires are at games for the benefit of the athletes. They must communicate their decisions to the athletes using their whistle and hand signals.

However, umpires are not at games to communicate with the coaches and there is nothing in the rules governing umpire conduct that holds the umpires accountable to communicate well with the coaches. In fact, the word coach doesn't even appear in the *Rules of Hockey* and the NFHS rules groups coaches with spectators in **Rule 12 Conduct of Coaches and Spectators**.

Second, suggesting that the umpires should be evaluated on whether they "communicate well with coaches" not only exposes a lack of rules knowledge (not a good thing for an umpire association to do) the question also demonstrates a level of arrogance with which none of us should be comfortable— not everyone speaks the same language. Perhaps the umpire and the coach speak different languages. How can anyone collect a feedback form with a question like that when coaches and umpires don't even speak the same language? Its presence would undermine what limited validity the process might hold.

A key role of every umpire association is to evaluate and advance the skills of its umpire members. If an association is considering collecting feedback from non-umpires, the association has to be careful not to give anyone the impression that it has given that responsibility away. Unless the association has a dedicated team of professionals to plan, execute, and monitor such a program, collecting feedback can easily do far more harm than good.

CHAPTER 9

BREAKING TIES

The first thing to know about tie breakers is that they are not part of the *Rules of Hockey*. Therefore, every governing body – whether it is a national governing body or a game hosted by a local recreation department – can make up whatever it wants to do (or not do) as a tiebreakers. Flipping a coin can be used to determine winners and not be a breach of the *Rules of Hockey*.

There are two types of tiebreakers commonly used to determine the outcome of a field hockey game.

1. Extra playing time with a reduced number of players in an "open field" competition (a.k.a. overtime)
2. A series of some type of set-play competitions

NOTE: The minutes played, shots taken, and goals scored in extra playing time are included in game and player statistics (see the chapter titled "Keeping Stats"). In short, for statistical purposes, extra playing time is not considered part of a tie breaker.

OPEN FIELD COMPETITIONS

The "open field" tiebreaker competitions are usually golden goal affairs (a.k.a. sudden victory) with seven players from each team competing under almost all the same rules that governed regulation. The one rule exception is that on Penalty Corners, a maximum of four defenders are allowed to begin from a position behind the back-line. During regulation, a maximum of five defenders are allowed to begin from a position behind the back-line.

This approach is mandated throughout the USA in the college system. Currently, the teams will contest in two 15-minute overtime periods until one team scores. As soon as a team scores, the tie is broken and the game is over. If neither team scores, a "set play" tiebreaker is used to try to determine a winner.

In almost every game I've seen that go into an open-field competition with a reduced number of players, almost all end very quickly on a breakaway opportunity (i.e. a one-on-one situation).

SET-PLAY COMPETITIONS

There are two popular "set play" competitions. Both feature an individual attacker attempting to score against an individual defender (i.e. a one-on-one situation).

As in baseball, scoring opportunities are given in innings. The team "at bat" sends an attacker to the plate, eh, stroke mark. The other team is on defense and the team on defense sends its goalkeeper to the goal. Unlike a nine inning baseball game, a field hockey tiebreaker usually only has five innings.

This type of tiebreaker is not determined by a golden goal but by the cumulative number of scores through the end of the competition (through the bottom of the fifth inning). If one team amasses an insurmountable score, the remaining innings are not played. If after five innings the score remains tied, another five innings might be played or a series single innings might be used to determine the winner.

There are almost always a minimum of five innings in every set-play tiebreaker but, I have seen as few as three when time constraints require it.

The two popular set-play competitions are:

1. Strokes – Uses the same rules that govern a Penalty Stroke, including how each of these one-on-one competitions is managed by the umpires. After the umpire blows his/her whistle, the attacker pushes or flicks the ball at the goal from 7 yards away from the middle of the goal-line. The goalkeeper begins with both feet on the goal-line and cannot come forward of the goal-line until the attacker plays the ball.

2. Shootout – Although the shootout has been described as a possible tiebreaker for decades in the back of the NFHS's rule book, most people think this type of one-on-one situation was recently invented. After the umpire blows his/her whistle, the attacker dribbles the ball into the circle from the center of the 25-yard line and must score from within the circle in less than a prescribed amount of time (typically 8 seconds). The goalkeeper begins on or behind the goal-line and cannot come forward of the goal-line until the attacker plays the ball and, just as on a Penalty Stroke, not on the umpire's starting whistle.

 UMPIRES – SHOOTOUT POSITIONING
During the shootout, umpires position themselves rather like they would during a Penalty Stroke.

The managing umpire is to the right of the attacker (left of the goalkeeper) and moves with the play just as one does when an attacker is on a breakaway.

The support umpire begins near the back-line, to the goalkeeper's right.

UMPIRES – SHOOTOUT RESPONSIBILITIES

Like on a Penalty Stroke, the managing umpire is responsible for all decisions. The support umpire's responsibility is to watch the play and answer any questions that the managing umpire might ask the support umpire and, just as on a Penalty Stroke, to be in position to help the managing umpire determine whether the ball has crossed the goal-line, both completely and before time expires.

UMPIRES – SHOOTOUT TIMING

Use of a visible countdown clock with automatic horn is best. The countdown must begin when the managing umpire blows his/her whistle to begin the shootout. If time will be kept manually, it is of critical importance that the timer does not watch (turns his/her back to) the Shoot Out so as not to be distracted by the action. The timer should signal the end of time with a loud audible device (whistle, air horn, etc.). In all cases, the timer should not change to ensure the highest level of consistency possible.

CHAPTER 10

KEEPING STATS

The KEEPING STATS chapter of Field Hockey: Understanding the Game was written by Chip Rogers and edited by Cris Maloney. For more information about official field hockey statistics, please contact Chip at chip.rogers@miamioh.edu.

NOTE: The instructions can be applied to all levels of field hockey through they were created to establish consistency within NCAA games. The feminine gender is used in this chapter for the reader's convenience.

With the rapid growth of the sport of field hockey, it is important that the recording of the statistics of the game, which serve as a permanent record of the contest, be accurate and be meaningful to anyone who reads them. To this end, it is important to have a compilation of the terms used in statistics.

The purpose of this chapter is to address this need of nomenclature for the statistics currently used. In addition, this chapter will help to establish some guidelines for consistency.

Consistency is a fundamental part of the taking of statistics. Consistency is important not only from game-to-game for an individual team but also from team to team so that statistics can be compared across teams. There are many situations in which players are compared on a statistical basis; it is crucial to a fair comparison that the statisticians that are with the various teams be of the same mindset.

In each of these explanations below, many examples are given as possible scenarios that a statistician might encounter. They are by no means exhaustive nor are they all-inclusive. They simply provide a means to demonstrate some situations and provide a guideline for the recording of the statistics. In each of the examples, members from Team A all have names that begin with the letter "A" and players on the opposing team, Team B, all have names that begin with the letter "B."

Following the description of each of the statistics, two special situations (shoot-out competition and a substitute goalkeeper) are described. Finally, a list of formulas is provided to reacquaint the statisticians with the method of determining such statistics as scoring offense, scoring defense, save percentage and goals against average.

The statistics described below are as follows:
- SHOT
  - Shot on Goal
- GOAL
  - Game-Winning Goal
- ASSIST
- SAVE (GOALKEEPER SAVE, DEFENSIVE SAVE)
- PENALTY CORNERS

The special situations are:
- SHOOT OUT COMPETITION
- INCOMPLETE GAMES
- NO GOALKEEPER (including using a player with goalkeeper privileges or an extra field player)
- FORFEIT

SHOT
A shot is any attempt made by a player to score a goal.

The player, regardless of her playing position on the field, must be playing the ball in such a manner that her actions could result in her scoring on the opposing team's goal. Where she is on the field, the speed of the shot, and the placement of the other players, both on her team and the opposing team, are irrelevant – if she can LEGALLY score a goal from her spot on the field.

A shot – one that is deemed to be legal – can have four outcomes: a goal, a save (for the opposing goalkeeper or a defender on the opposing team), it can go wide, or a foul can be assessed to the opposing team.

If a player takes a shot that is blocked by a player who is in front of the goalkeeper, the shot still counts and is just considered wide. If the player is behind the goalkeeper or the goalkeeper is out of position to make the save (not a testament to her ability, just a note to determine viability of a defensive save), the player who stops the ball from going in the net shall be credited with a defensive save (see below).

Note that an attempt that is broken up by a foul (e.g. hits the body of a defending player, hits the wrong side of the stick of a defending player) should still be considered a shot.

If an attacking player enters the circle and directs the ball towards the cage, and brings out the goalkeeper to make a play on the ball, the intervention of the goalkeeper will often be the determining factor in crediting a shot.

It is important to note that a "shot" taken outside the circle should not be credited as a shot because if it goes in the cage untouched, it would not count as a goal.

Also, a shot that is deemed dangerous (e.g. on a direct corner) is not a shot since it cannot score.

Shot On Goal

Any shot attempt that results in either a save (goalkeeper or defensive) or a goal. *Note that shots on goal are preferable to record than shots.*

GOAL

In all cases, the last player on the attacking team who touches the ball inside the circle before it crosses the goal-line shall be credited with the score. A goal should only be recorded if the umpire signals a goal is scored.

There are situations in which the ball might cross the goal-line but the goal is disallowed for various reasons, including a shot that is deemed dangerous. A goal cannot be disallowed after the center-pass is taken that follows the apparent goal. It is crucial that a goal not be recorded until the umpire gives the signal and the center-pass is taken

NOTE: Goals are recorded as time into in the game.

Examples of Goals

- Amanda strikes the ball in the circle and sends it on a path to the cage. Betty attempts to block the shot, but her attempt does not stop the progress of the ball. Betty redirected the ball but it crossed the goal-line. A goal shall be awarded to Amanda

- On a Penalty Corner, the ball is passed outside the circle and Ali takes the ball to the circle-line. She shoots and the hits a defender's leg, including the goalkeeper, before the ball crosses the goal-line. The goal shall be awarded to Ali
- Ammie dribbles towards the goal along the backline. She enters the circle and passes the ball to a teammate in front of the cage. The teammate misses the pass but the ball is directed across the goal-line after hitting the back of a defender's stick, the defender's body, the goalkeeper's pads, the goalkeeper's helmet, or an umpire's body. Ammie shall get credit for a goal

Note that starting in 2014, own goals have been taken out of the game.

NOTE: A goal should be recorded as "player-up" if the defending team has been penalized with a card (green, yellow or red).

Game-Winning Goal (GWG)
The game-winning goal is the goal that puts a team ahead for good. If Team A is up 4-0 and Team B scores a late goal to make it 4-1, the GWG is the first goal scored by Team A. If Team B pulls to 4-3, it is still the first goal by Team A.

ASSIST
An assist is a play that directly results in a goal being scored.

NOTE: Only on a Penalty Corner can more than one assist be given.

The assist is a pass made by one teammate to another who in turn scores a goal. It is imperative that the statistician exercises consistent and clear judgment in awarding an assist. It should be noted that an assist does not detract from the player who scored a goal; that is, an unassisted goal is no better statistically than an assisted goal. However, not every goal needs to be assisted. Consistency remains the underlying principle with this statistic.

Specific situations include but are not limited to:

- **Breakaway situation:** Amanda, a forward, is playing at the midfield stripe. Her teammate Abbie, a back, intercepts a pass and Amanda takes off downfield uncontested. Abbie slots the ball through to Amanda 30 yards from the goal and Amanda dribbles and scores without a defensive player marking her. Even though Amanda took more than three steps, Abbie set up the play that allowed her team to score. The yardstick is the defensive pressure that Amanda faces in her scoring run. If Amanda must outrace/perform excessive defensive pressure, she will record an unassisted goal

- **Odd-woman rush:** Amanda picks up a loose ball and races down field with Alix on her side. The only defensive pressure is Barbara, at goalkeeper, who must cover both players. Barbara moves out to play the ball, leaving Alix free. Amanda passes Alix the ball and Alix takes 4 or 5 steps before shooting. If Alix scores, Amanda is awarded an assist.

NOTE: *An assist should not be given if the goal-scorer creates the goal herself. For this reason, it is imperative that a statistician not only is consistent with his or her recording but also has a good understanding of the game and its play.*

An assist is NOT awarded to a player that shoots and has her shot rebound off the post or the goalkeeper and the ball is picked up by a teammate and shot in the goal.

Example

Agnes shoots and her shot caroms off the pads of the goalkeeper. Amory collects the ball and scores on a scramble in front of the cage. Agnes is not awarded an assist; she is credited with a shot (the goalkeeper gets a save) and Amory gets a shot and a goal

SINGLE ASSISTS

Single assists include, but are not limited to:

- A goal scored by a tip or a deflection by a player on the attacking team
- A pass from either the Striker or the Stick Stop to a player on either side of the Battery

DOUBLE ASSISTS

There is **only ONE** instance in which two people can be awarded an assist on a goal, and it takes place during a Penalty Corner.

Terms related to the attacking team on a Penalty Corner:

ACTIONS
Insertion*: The action of putting the ball into play to begin the Penalty Corner*
Direct Shot*: A shot taken during a Penalty Corner without any pass except for the ball being Inserted or positioned by the Stick Stop*

PERSONNEL
Inserter*: The attacker who starts the Penalty Corner from the back-line, i.e. the player who inserts the ball into play*
Stick Stop*: The attacker who receives the inserted ball and positions the ball for the Striker or passes to another attacker*
Striker*: The attacker who on a Penalty Corner who is likely to take the first shot after the ball is received by themselves or the Stick Stop*
Battery/Castle*: Two attackers – a Stick Stop and Striker – who are in close proximity to each other and appear ready to receive and shoot the ball. Teams sometimes setup multiple batteries to help confuse their opponents*

If a player scores on a Direct Shot during a Penalty Corner, then the Inserter and Stick Stop may be credited with an assist. If there is any other kind of play, then only the person with the final pass may be credited with an assist, i.e. a Single Assist.

NOTE: In open field play and on a Penalty Corner, if the ball is deflected by a defensive player and the ball crosses the goal-line, the assist(s) are given as if that ball had not touched a defending player. Thus, if a direct shot on a Penalty Corner is last touched by a defensive player, both the Inserter and the Stick Stop get the assists, and the goal is given to the attacker who played the ball just prior to the defender's deflection. i.e. the Striker. If just a single assist would normally be awarded had the ball gone directly into the goal instead of being last touched by a defensive player, the single assist is still given.

SAVE: The save records each time a player stops a ball from going across the goal-line her team is defending that if she did not stop, would result in a score for the opponent.

Obviously, each time the ball completely passes the plane of the goal-line a goal is scored when the ball is touched by the attack inside the circle, did not otherwise leave the circle, and there is not a violation by the attack prior to the ball crossing the goal-line (dangerous shot, use of the back of the stick, hard forehand edge hit, etc.). However, there are situations in which a ball that advances in a scoring manner and the goalkeeper does not record a save. In looking at the definition of a goal, in which an offensive player has played the ball inside the scoring circle, one finds the basis for the definition of a save. A goalkeeper should get credit for a save only if they stop a ball from going in the goal after it has been touched by an attacker in the circle and the ball is headed towards the goal. It does not matter who touched it last as long as it was touched by an attacker in the circle; the goalkeeper still records a save if she stops it from going in the net.

A statistician should use reasonable guidance to award a save; if, from an elevated, angled position of sight, a shot might appear to be headed just wide of the goal, but the goalkeeper stops it, a save can be awarded.

There CANNOT be more saves recorded than shots for the opponent. In addition, a shot that hits the crossbar or post is not recorded as a save for the goalkeeper.

Examples

- Amanda takes a shot that would go in. Brittany, the goalkeeper, blocks the shot. Brittany records a save; Amanda records a shot
- Agnes is the striker on a Penalty Corner. Her shot, which is ruled "safe," is saved by Brittany from going in the cage. Brittany's save, however, pops up and the umpire rules a lifted or dangerous ball and awards team A another corner. Brittany's save is still a save, as she prevented the ball from going into the goal
- Ammie is on a breakaway and dribbles into the circle. Brittany comes out to play her and blocks the ball after Ammie has taken it into the circle and sent it towards the cage. Because an offensive player has touched the ball inside the circle, Brittany gets credit for the save. Note that Ammie also gets credit for a shot as well
- Alice carries the ball into the circle and attempts a pass to Annie, but the pass is tipped up by Belle and redirected towards the cage. Brittany dives to stop the ball from going in the cage, as should the ball cross the line, it would be a goal. Brittany gets a save; Alice records a shot

DEFENSIVE SAVE

On a corner Amory shoots the ball in the corner away from the goalkeeper. Barb, who is on the post, legally stops the ball from going in the cage. Amory gets credit for a shot, and Barb records a defensive save.

NOTE: A defensive player who is playing in front of the goalkeeper who blocks a shot IS NOT credited with a defensive save. The defensive save must be the FINAL ABSOLUTE last line of defense.

Examples

The following are situations in which the goalkeeper plays the ball but there is NOT a save:

- A pass from inside the circle coming across the mouth of the cage that the goalkeeper intercepts and clears the ball out of the circle (or away from play)
- The goalkeeper blocks a crossing pass from outside the circle that is not directed towards the goal as a shot

The only judgment call that should be made in the recording of a save is whether the ball would have gone in the cage. It is rare for a team to have 100% accuracy in shot placement; thus, it would be unusual for a team to have as many saves (and goals against) as the opponent has shots. Again, a crucial point is that a shot that hits the post is not considered a save.

It is important that a statistician keep careful account of all of the shots during a game; for this purpose, a table for recording shots should account for each team's shots that hit posts and go wide of the goal, in addition to each team's total number of shots.

SHUTOUTS

A goalkeeper can only get credit for a shutout if:

- Her team holds the opponent scoreless
- She plays the entire game in which there is open play on the field – tiebreakers such as a 7v7 are included in crediting a goalkeeper with a shutout, however, set-play tiebreakers (such as Penalty Corners, Penalty Strokes, Shoot Outs) are not
- She is suspended or substituted and replaced on the field with a goalkeeper or a player with goalkeeping privileges

NOTE: *Teams that split their goalkeeper are credited with a shutout, but the goalkeepers involved are not credited with a "half-shutout."*

When a game that ends 0-0, after regulation and overtime, both team's goalkeepers shall record a shutout if they played the entire game, regardless of the result in a set-play tiebreaker.

Example
A team could lose a game by a recorded final score of 1-0 as the result of the team's performance in a shootout, but the goalkeeper, if she played the entire game including any open-play overtime period(s), would record a shutout

PENALTY CORNERS
Commonly called corners, short corners, and even "shorties" in some parts of the world, Penalty Corners are awarded by umpires for certain infractions by the defense depending on the type of breach and where the breach takes place.

Goals scored off deflections by a defensive stick should be awarded to the offensive player who last touched the ball.

If the defense breaks early and the umpire resets the Penalty Corners, a new Penalty Corners shall not be recorded; for statistical purposes it is the same Penalty Corners in count of Penalty Corners awarded.

A direct shot on a Penalty Corners is the only situation in which a double assist can be awarded. Care should be noted that it is a direct strike, and not a deflected/tipped ball, in which case the sole assist would go to the striker with the goal going to the attacking player who deflected the ball in.

SPECIAL FIELD HOCKEY SITUATIONS
The shootout competition: In the case that Team A and Team B are tied following the mandatory, sudden-victory 10 minutes overtime periods, a shootout competition is held to determine a winner of the contest. Teams go through one series of a best of five, played to completion, unless one team has a

decided advantage. If after a set of five both teams are tied, a sudden victory set of five is taken until a winner has been declared. The team that wins the contest will be awarded a "team goal" to be added to the score of that team. The result is recorded as such: Team A defeats Team B in a shootout OR "A, 2-1 SO."

It is important to note that each team is only held accountable for the goals scored in regulation (in the example above, just the one goal). **The game-winning "goal" is not charged to the other team; it is not allowed by anyone, nor is it scored by anyone.** In stats-recording programs (e.g. StatCrew) the "goal" is scored by "team" and it should not be included in total goals scored on the season. It should also not be included in total goals allowed.

NOTE: If a player participates in the shootout, she is considered to have participated in the game.

The goalkeeper of record in the game are the keepers who participate in the shootout. She might or might not be the goalkeeper who played during regulation. Since the teams are tied at the end of regulation, the goalkeeper of the team that loses is the one who was in when her team went behind for good, which is the definition of the goalkeeper of record.

NOTE: If two teams enter a shootout with the score tied at 0-0, BOTH goalkeepers are awarded a shutout.

Should an attempt result in a stroke, and a different player attempts the stroke, the ORIGINAL player who attempted the shootout is recorded, not the person who takes the stroke.

When there is no goalkeeper: In games that do not require a team to have a goalkeeper on the field, teams may elect to play an extra field player. From a statistical standpoint, the situation is treated the same; that is, there is NO goalkeeper on the field. Goals are charged to the team, but NOT charged to any goalkeeper.

A keeper's minutes should reflect only the time she is on the field. The goal should be recorded with an Empty Net (en) to reflect that the goal was scored without a fully kitted goalkeeper.

Examples

- Team A leads 1-0 and Team B pulls their keeper with 4:00 to play. Brittany comes off the field while a field player named Betsy enters the game. Team A scores with 2:00 to play. Brittany is charged with only one goal against in 56 minutes of play, while Team B overall has two goals against during the 60-minute game. Team A's goal should be listed as an Empty Net (en) goal to reflect the actual situation, because to list the goal against a field player is a misleading statistic

- Team A leads 2-0 and Team B pulls their keeper with 10:00 to play. Brittany comes off the field while a field player named Betsy enters the game. On a breakaway, Team A advances the ball upfield and Ammie shoots as soon as she enters the circle. Betsy dives and knocks the ball away from the cage with her stick. On the ensuing long hit, Team A is able to score. Brittany is charged with only one goal against in 50 minutes of play, while Team B overall has three goals against during the 60-minute game. Team A's goal should be listed as an Empty Net (en) goal to reflect the actual situation, but Betsy is credited with a save

GOALKEEPER OF RECORD

In general, the goalkeeper of record in the game is the one who is in the cage when the relative score changes for good. That is, if Team A scores in the first minute of play and takes a 1-0 lead, and they do not relinquish the lead all game, the goalkeepers who were in the game when the team went up (or down) 1-0 are recorded, even if the score changes dramatically throughout the course of the contest. If the relative score remains the same, they are the goalkeepers of record.

INCOMPLETE GAMES
In the case that the game ends prior to completion, the game is not considered official and therefore the stats of the games are not official. Note that a contest cannot end in a tie; the teams must go through the tie-breaking procedures (overtime and/or shootout) to break the tie. If the game is suspended by the umpires and cannot be made up that day, it may be picked up at the point of interruption. If the game is not continued, it is not completed and therefore the stats cannot be included.

FORFEIT
There is no forfeit of a contest until both participating teams are present and the umpire or other appropriate contest official has assumed jurisdiction in accordance with the applicable playing rules. When a team does not appear, e.g., due to weather conditions, accidents, breakdown of vehicles, illness or catastrophic causes, a forfeit is not recorded. An institution shall not, for statistical purposes, declare a forfeit for non-fulfillment of a contract. Such instances shall be considered "no contest".

In circumstances involving institutions from the same conference, the league office has the option to declare a forfeit win and loss for conference-standings purposes, but this does not change an institution's overall won-lost record.

Examples
- Should a game result in a forfeit, the final score of the game shall be recorded as 1-0 for the team accepting the forfeit. The goal scored is recorded as a team goal; it is not scored by an individual. Nor is the goal "allowed" included in a team's countable goals for the season. None of the statistics generated in the game are to be recorded

- Should a game be called by an umpire due to the failure of a coach who has been booked with a red card to leave the playing area, the score shall be recorded as 1-0. However, all the statistics awarded in the game shall be counted as recorded. A team shall not be penalized statistics due to the actions of an opposing coach

By no means are those two examples perfect nor are they exhaustive. They only represent some of the more common situations and give an idea of how a statistician should record the play. In any situation where a question arises; it is crucial that the statisticians of both teams discuss the situation so that both teams' statistics are identical.

For those using computer-generated stats programs:
- make sure all times set are for field hockey
- make sure the title lists "field hockey" and NOT "soccer"
- there are no such things as penalty shots. There are Penalty Corners and Penalty Strokes, but no penalty shots
- shootout competitions are separate statistically from the rest of the game with regard to saves and goals scored

Note: In the game summary, it is perfectly fine to say that a goalkeeper made saves in a set-play tiebreaker (shootout, strokes, etc.), but they are not recorded in her overall totals, nor are the shots against or the goals recorded.

STATISTICAL FORMULAS
Presented formulas are for 60-minute games and do not include any overtime period(s). Adjust formulas accordingly for total minutes played. Do not include set-play tiebreakers.

SCORING AVERAGE (Scoring offense)	<u>Number of goals x 60</u> Number of minutes played Team A has played 15 games (one OT of 5 min) and scored 60 goals. 60x60=3,600 15x60+5=905 3600/905=3.98 gpg Team A has a scoring offense of 3.98 gpg
SCORING DEFENSE	<u>Number of goals allowed x60</u> Number of minutes played Team A's opponents have scored 25 goals. 25x60=1,500 1500/905=1.66 Team A has a scoring defense of 1.66
SCORING MARGIN	Scoring Average-Scoring Defense=Scoring Margin
SAVE PERCENTAGE	<u>Number of saves</u> Number of saves+ Number of goals Anna has made 180 saves and has allowed 75 goals. 180+75=255 180/255=0.706 Anna's save percentage is 0.706

GOALS AGAINST AVERAGE (GAA)	Number of goals allowed x 60 Total minutes played Anna has allowed 20 goals while playing in 985 minutes. 20x60=1200 1200/985=1.22 Anna has a GAA of 1.22. Notice that the team has played 905 minutes; she has played 93.4% of the team's minutes. Her GAA is very close to the scoring defense.
CAREER GAA	When goalkeepers play in a mix of 60- and 70-minute games during their career, determining Career GAA should be calculated using the following formula: A+B/total minutes played Where A = number of goals allowed in a 60-minute game x 60, and B = number of goals allowed in a 70-minute game x 70. For example: Anna has allowed 10 goals in 5 games of 60 minutes and played 280 minutes of the 300 minutes available. She also allowed 10 goals in 5 games of 70 minutes and played 300 minutes of the 350 minutes available. Therefore, Anna's Career GAA is 2.24. 10x60+10x70 = 1300/(280+300) = 2.24 IT IS NOT: 20x70 = 1400/580 = 2.41

CHAPTER 11

WISDOM

"Wisdom is knowing what to do next, skill is knowing how to do it, and virtue is doing it."

– David Starr Jordan, educator and peace activist (past president of Indiana University and Stanford University)

I've learned many things in more than 30 years of officiating hockey. As is life, learning what not to do largely comes from having done the absolute wrong thing. Even not doing some things takes skill, or courage. So, if I might be so bold as to argue the point with Dr. Jordan, sometimes virtue includes not doing it.

Umpire is Not Spelled "B-A-L-L B-O-Y"

Once the game has begun, umpires should NEVER touch the ball. They should pretend it is poisonous if they have to but they should NOT touch the ball. Umpires are not ball boys and ball girls. Umpires are there to do one thing, officiate—not pick up the hockey ball during time-outs, between periods or at the end of the game. Umpires are not at games to chase after the hockey ball if it goes out of bounds, get the ball prior to a Penalty Stroke, or pick it up after an injury time-out. The ONLY exception for this aspect of the "Maloney Code of Conduct" is that if the umpire is outside the lines of the competition surface and the hockey ball is rolling out of bounds AND it will otherwise hit the umpire in the foot, then and only then, the umpire doesn't have to get out of the way. Still, it is virtuous NOT to touch the ball.

Echoing Whistles

An umpire should NOT whistle simply because the other umpire has whistled. A second whistle, by the umpire who did not whistle first, is only helpful when the athletes have continued to compete and didn't realize they should stop!

Simultaneous Whistles

During the course of a hockey game umpires will invariably blow their whistle at the exact same moment, both thinking they are the umpire who should make the call. It is bound to happen, especially at lower levels of the game and it typically happens near the grey area, purposefully drawn imprecisely, indicated in the following graphic.

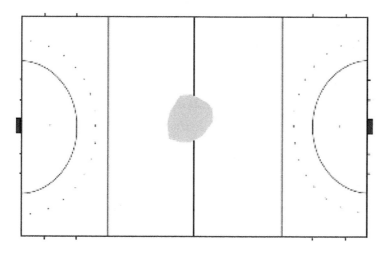

That's not so bad and it is to be expected. The bad news, however, is when both umpires end up pointing in opposite directions.

 UMPIRES: If you find you're in a situation where both umpires have blown their whistle AND you can wait half a second to see which way the other umpire is pointing— point that way too! At the moment it happens, do a quick sanity check as to who should have made the call. If the play was heading toward you, the other umpire should not give direction, you should (and vice versa). This all happens in a tenth of a second but, it's not that hard.

If the direction of the play doesn't determine which call should be acted on and both umpires have signaled in opposite directions, then the position of the ball on the competition surface should be used as the determining factor. Use the center-line to divide the competition surface and the call should 'go to' the umpire who has responsibility for the circle that is in that half of the competition surface.

This should hardly ever happen. Resolving it can be a little sloppy. The umpires must, before allowing play to resume, make absolutely sure that the team that ends up defending against the restart is adequately prepared to begin.

 UMPIRES: If you're about to blow your whistle for possession to your right but the other umpire blows his or her whistle first, DON'T also blow yours...even when you see that the other umpire is signaling that the direction will be to your left. It is best to sort out any remaining disagreements about such situations during a break than with "dueling arms" from opposite sides of the competition surface. If, however, you feel the difference is important, call a time-out and get it right—right then and there. This is easy for umpires who are familiar working with each other.

I will often put my arm down as quickly as I can when I hear the second whistle, especially if play was in the grey area at mid-field, and point in whatever direction the other umpire has indicated.

 UMPIRES: Showing the world that you and your partner are in agreement will pay big dividends throughout the game (and even into future games).

The Perils of Verbalizing Calls

Umpires should not verbalize their calls. An occasional, *"Red ball,"* is okay especially if the umpire gets turned around and they're not sure which way the Red team is going (happens a lot when the teams switch ends). That is understandable and a service to everyone involved (it shouldn't be relied upon).

 UMPIRES: When forced to call a color, don't say both teams' colors. For example don't say, "Red ball. Off Blue." And, don't say, "Red ball," one time and "Off Blue," the next. Always say who has it or who doesn't. Keep it consistent.

It is NOT okay to shout out things like, *"Obstruction"*, *"Corner"*, or *"Free Hit."* Why not? The following is a true story.

An umpire who constantly verbalized her calls was officiating a game involving team X for the third game in a row. When this umpire calls a Penalty Corner she blows her whistle and barks, *"Corner."* In the third game, team X was defending as team Y brought the ball into the circle. The attack passed the ball into the circle and it struck the lower leg of one of the defenders. The umpire held for advantage. One of the attackers, however, yelled out, *"Corner!"* Again, the defenders from team X had just played their two previous games with this verbalizing umpire and every last one of the defenders stood up and relaxed, reacting like a dog in a Pavlovian experiment hearing a bell ring before dinner, thinking that a Penalty Corner had been called. One of the attackers hit the ball into the goal with a weak shot from 14 yards away. The umpire signaled the goal.

That's a great example of why we tell the athletes to, *"Play to the whistle,"* but if you had become used to the verbalizing umpire and you heard, *"Corner!"* you would almost certainly stop too, just as if you had heard the whistle.

NOTE: *The umpire should have disallowed the goal and carded the attacking team for misconduct.*

Verbalizing calls is a very slippery slope.

I've seen umpires verbally scold players from a distance. They end up shouting at the athletes. Scolding a player is NOT acceptable, whether from the other end of the competition surface or in a private conversation that no one else can hear. Umpires should use their cards, not their mouth, if something 'harsh' has to be said.

UMPIRES: When you are carding an athlete, you can certainly tell them why they are being carded but just share the facts and save the sermon.

Other reasons umpires don't want to verbalize their calls is that:

- When you open your mouth, you're inviting other people to open theirs

- It could just be that the players don't speak the umpire's native language

- The more the umpire says, the more likely it is that they'll:

  ❖ Say something that is wrong or

  ❖ Say something that can be taken out of context

 UMPIRES: Remember, nowadays, you ARE being recorded. You don't want to end up the star of a YouTube video saying something silly or mean do you?

Umpires want to do almost ALL of their public speaking with their whistle and arm signals. Short, friendly private comments—even if done to deliver a friendly caution—are appropriate (especially if the umpire and the athlete share a common language).

 UMPIRES: Just because you're officiating in country X doesn't mean that every athlete in the game speaks the dominant language in country X. Just because you're officiating in the USA doesn't mean all the players speak English. And, remember not every player can hear. Before you speak, think of what you would say if you brought an athlete over to card and learned that he or she was completely deaf?

CHAPTER *12*

QUIZ YOURSELF

"Consistency is the last refuge of the unimaginative."

– Oscar Wilde

That's a disruptive thought for umpires, isn't it? After all, we live and die by consistency and here, Oscar Wilde insults us for achieving one of our goals.

I believe there can be serious, positive benefits from disruptive thinking, disruptive technology, and other disruptive changes that shift the way we think and act. Some argue that we should only seek incremental changes. I strongly believe that incremental change changes nothing. I'm not particularly comfortable in taking small steps when the destination is known and the route is clear.

Back in early 1980's, more than a few high school coaches were telling athletes not to use the reverse stick skill and NEVER hold the stick with one hand. That's like telling right handed basketball athletes that they aren't allowed to learn how to dribble with the left hand. Why was this acceptable in hockey? Why was it considered disruptive coaching to require kids to develop one-handed and backhand skills?

I started testing a new teaching technique for kids as young as 8 years old by teaching them to ONLY use a backhand, one handed dribble. The kids demonstrated that they developed hockey skills much more rapidly than I had seen in kids who I had coached previously. A year later I was invited to present this approach at an International Olympic Committee solidarity seminar for hockey coaching.

I tell you this story because I'm inviting you to find fault with this book. Use what you can but find your own way to be the very best umpire, player, coach, fan you can be. Don't limit yourself to only one way of thinking. Challenge yourself when you're feeling comfortable about what you're doing. Don't be complacent. Disrupt your way of thinking!

 UMPIRES: Try to poke holes in my advice, get other coaching, find fault with what everyone tells you as a means of creating your own path to success. I don't care if you do what I say, this book isn't about me, it's about you. I only care that you become the best umpire you can be and that your officiating helps to advance hockey.

No matter what your career, doubting things you are certain about, challenging your preconceived notions, and questioning your current understanding, even privately questioning the coaching you receive—those behaviors will help to make you more creative and self-assured, allowing you to transcend the amount of access you have to high level instructors.

Be disruptive to your personal status quo. Think creatively. Work hard. Make yourself better.

Maloney's Colorful Hockey Quiz

QUESTION #1: The teams competing in today's game are from a rivalry that dates back many years. This year, the Blue Devils (dressed in their blue shirts and blue socks), is heavily favored to win. The underdog's school is hosting the game.

The grass on the competition surface has just been cut and the surface is freshly lined and perfect in every measure. It's a bright sunny day and a cool breeze is pushing fall's first leaves across the ground.

The Red Riders are the underdogs but have welcomed the Blue Devils and are determined and excited about today's competition. The Red Riders look ready! They not only have on their game faces, they're wearing their brand new, bright red shirts and matching socks.

The umpires have finished their warmup, checked the goals, and are meeting at the center of the competition surface. Everything seems perfect.

Suddenly, the Blue Devils coach storms over to the umpires with rulebook in hand and an animated discussion ensues. The players looking on can see the Blue team coach shaking her head and repeatedly pointing to a page in the open rulebook. This does not look good.

What is the coach most likely talking about?

QUESTION #2: After that situation is resolved, the game begins.

A player on the Red team has been fouled and is about to take the Free Hit near the center-line. She's new to the sport and, foolishly, doesn't look behind her to see that her teammate is wide open and could easily receive the pass. In fact, she hasn't even looked up—she just puts the ball down in front of her and is getting ready to smack the ball as hard as she can.

She swings horribly, miss-hits the ball and the ball trickles forward about two feet and stops.

Can you predict, with absolute certainty, which team will have possession next and explain why (why not)?

QUESTION #3: Surprisingly, the Red Riders are dominating play early in the game.

A Red attacker has the ball in the circle and fakes a shot to the goalkeeper's stick side and instead shoots to the opposite side of the goal. The ball rises quickly to the upper corner of the goal.

The Blue Devils' goalkeeper reaches and makes a tremendous glove save, deflecting the ball just wide of the goal and over the back-line.

Draw a hockey competition surface, note the goal the blue goalkeeper is defending and show where, exactly, the ball will be put into play and by writing 'Red' or 'Blue' near the ball, identify which team will restart play.

QUESTION #4: A player from the Red Riders breaks away with the ball and enters the circle.

In desperation, a Blue Devils' player tries to tackle the attacker from behind, hacks her stick and the ball rolls over the backline. A Penalty Stroke is called but the Red Riders have not converted on a Penalty Stroke in more than a year.

The player approaching to take the shot on goal has only come into the game a few minutes ago. She's tall and, for what it's worth, her walk is not particularly graceful. Her long black hair is so thick and curly that it obscures most of her number as it makes it way down her back, nearly reaching the bottom of her bright green shirt.

Will the umpires allow this player to take the stroke? (Why/Why not?)

QUESTION #5: The Blue Devils' attack has settled down and has really taken charge.

It's near the end of the first half and once again the Blue Devils' attack has entered the Red Riders' circle! A Penalty Corner is earned and the Blue team is setting up to put the ball into play.

The Red Riders' goalkeeper has been absolutely amazing and her team, which should be down by about five goals, is behind by only one. She's already turned back three shots on Penalty Corners that were faster than the crowd has ever seen.

The tension on the sidelines is palpable. The fans turn their attention to the scoreboard as they've just realized it is counting down the final few seconds of the first half. A roar builds as the fans for the Blue team start yelling and screaming, *"Hurry!"*

Perhaps confused by all the noise, the Blue team captain, who happens to be the player who will put the ball into play and was almost ready to begin, decides it would be best to start the Penalty Corner from the other side of the goal. She picks up the ball and sprints to the other side of the goal.

The crowd explodes but there is nothing they can do! Before she even puts the ball down time expires.

As the players walk off the competition surface to the team areas for half-time, the scorekeeper marks in the book that the score is tied. Both umpires see this, agree that the score is correct, and do nothing to change the entry.

How is this possible?

QUESTION #6: The umpire nearer the scorer's table blows the whistle to signal to start the second half of the game. After the whistle but before the ball is put into play by the Red Riders, the Red Riders' right wing starts running at a full sprint for the goal. Seeing this, a wing for the Blue Devils on the far side of the competition surface jumps across the center-line and sprints towards the other circle. The Red Riders still haven't put the ball into play.

Can the Blue Devils do this?

QUESTION #7: The Red team has a 2 to 1 lead over the Blue team as the game nears completion.

A Red Rider player swings at the ball to clear it from the circle. Her swing misses the ball and as she brings her stick back to swing again, she hits the ball with the back of her stick.

The lead official immediately blows the whistle and signals a Penalty Corner for the Blue Devils.

The Blue team takes the Penalty Corner. The hit comes off the back-line perfectly and races along the ground to the Blue player who will do a stick stop. The player uses the flat side of her stick to stop the ball perfectly on the circle line. A Blue teammate, who earned the nickname "Big Country" when she was in middle school, strikes the ball where it is and sends it so fast that it seemed to disappear before beating the goalkeeper's left foot.

The ball rattles the boards in the corner of the goal and the sound reverberates in the air until the cheers of the Blue team and their fans overwhelm it. The umpire signals goal and the teams head back to their positions for the center pass.

There were NO fouls by either team during the Penalty Corner and, happily, no other cards were issued during or after the game.

As the sun sinks lower in the late September sky, the game ends in regulation time with the score 2 - 1; the Red team won.

How is this possible?

WANT TO CHECK YOUR ANSWERS?

If you would like the answers to these questions, please visit:

UmpireHockey.com/answers

13

RESOURCES

Continuing to develop your skills as a hockey player, coach, and umpire (even as a knowledgeable fan) is critical to your long-term success and enjoyment of the game. Please make use of these additional resources.

BolsterHockey.com

Field hockey products, selected and some created by the author, for schools, clubs, players, goalkeepers, and umpires.

NFHS.org

If and only if you are based in the United States, you'll want to know about the NFHS (National Federation of State High School Associations). It is a member organization made up of state associations, which are in turn made up of member high schools (mostly public). The NFHS governs interscholastic field hockey competitions between its member high schools. If you want to contact the state association near you, the NFHS website has contact information and links to each state association.

UmpireHockey.com

The UmpireHockey.com site is dedicated to officiating hockey. Visit the site to learn about and enroll in my online course for new and experienced umpires. The **High-Performance Umpiring & Rules™** course is the official training course for multiple umpire associations and has been taken by students in twenty states and in five countries.

USAFieldHockey.com

This is the site of the national governing body for hockey in the USA. No matter what country you play, coach, or officiate in, join your national association!

Other Books of Possible Interest

- Art of Sports Officiating by Kathryn L. Davis

- Psychology of Officiating by Robert S. Weinberg and Peggy A. Richardson

- The Art of Officiating Sports by John William Bunn

- Hockey in the Blood by Gavin Featherstone

- Field Hockey: The Beginner's Guide by Cris Maloney

ABOUT THE AUTHOR

After participating in Track & Field in middle school and high school, earning All American status as a member of a national record setting shuttle hurdle relay team, Mr. Maloney began playing field hockey while in college. He became a nationally certified umpire in 1977. In the 1980s he pursued development and coaching activities, founding New Jersey's Garden State Games Field Hockey Event, serving as an assistant coach to two gold medal winning teams in United States Olympic Committee national sporting events, and attending an Olympic Solidarity Coaching seminar offered by the International Olympic Committee where he presented his paper titled *Field Hockey: The First 30-Minutes*.

Maloney wrote the first edition of this book, originally titled *How To Umpire Field Hockey*, in 2001 and began focusing on umpire training. He became a nationally certified Level II Umpire Coach and started working with USA Field Hockey to help improve the standard of umpiring across the country. In 2013 he was commissioned by USA Field Hockey to write his second book, *JUMP IN! A Beginner's Guide To Field Hockey Umpiring*.

Always an innovator, in 2003 Maloney was the first field hockey assigner to recommend and use web-based technology to assign umpires to games. In 2009, the same technology was purchased by New Jersey's high school athletic association (the NJSIAA) for use by high school assigners in all sports. He was also first, in 2005, to recommend, use, and supervise the use of walkie-talkies during high school games. In 2012 the use of walkie-talkies was officially endorsed by the National Federation of State High School Associations. In 2013 he organized the first Hockey5s league in the USA.

Maloney is the publisher of UmpireHockey.com, produces videos about the rules governing field hockey, is the creator and editor of the *Ask the Umpire* feature on USA Field Hockey's website, teaches umpiring courses, makes presentations helping umpires, coaches, players, and parents understand the sport of field hockey. More than 200 students in five countries have enrolled in his online rules and umpire training course (UmpireHockey.com/enroll). In 2018 he published *Field Hockey: The Beginner's Guide*, which provides a high-level overview of the sport. Maloney also runs programs to introduce field hockey to boys and girls in central New Jersey.

Made in the USA
Las Vegas, NV
29 September 2022